mug cakes

mug cakes

SPEEDY MICROWAVE TREATS
TO SATISFY YOUR SWEET TOOTH

Leslie Bilderback

PHOTOGRAPHS BY TERI LYN FISHER

St. Martin's Griffin / New York

This book is dedicated to all the CS's in the United States Navy—

those I have taught, and those I have yet to teach

through the Adopt-a-Ship program.

Thanks for welcoming me aboard.

contents

4: KIDS' STUFF

5: ADULTS ONLY

6: CHOC-O-RAMA

7: A LITTLE FRUITY

8: NUTS TO YOU

9: CELEBRATE!

introduction

If there's anything on earth that can bring a smile faster than a piece of cake, it's a cake you can make in five minutes.

The idea of making a cake in the microwave will certainly be poo-pooed by the professionals. But this is not a book to help you gain a spot on the Culinary Olympic team. This book is here to fulfill the cake craving you have after a long day at work, or in the middle of the night, or when the plumber presents you with a $900 invoice.

This book is also here to quash all preconceived notions you have about baking. Pastry chefs have long touted pastry as a "science." Well, yes, it is. But so is cooking a chicken, planting a sunflower seed, balancing your checkbook, and changing the oil in your car. That it is a science does not mean only the professionally trained can do it, nor does it mean that it is too difficult for you to understand. Pastry chefs long ago perpetuated this idea so they could feel more important. And every time a cook is too afraid to try baking, those fossilized pastry chefs and their arrogant egotism win. So don't be intimidated! There is no better way to stick it to those bygone bakers than to create fabulous desserts in a mug, in a microwave, in five minutes.

Most of all, this book is here to stimulate your creative appetite, and get you in the kitchen making great cakes from scratch. There are hundreds of ideas here to get you started. And once you see how easy these cakes are, and you grasp the idea that baking is no big deal, please continue the exploration on your own. Try things. Combine things. Experiment. What have you got to lose? Baking ingredients are cheap. If you make a mistake, no harm, no foul. Just try again.

1

mug cake basics

Cake batter is cake batter, whether it is intended for a wedding cake or a microwaveable mug. Volume is the difference, and since this book is dedicated to cakes on a very small scale, a few things must be taken into consideration.

MUGS

Most of the recipes in this book are written for two mugs. That is because there is no standard mug size. When creating these recipes, an average mug, like the one you get at a coffee shop, was the base of reference. That said, most of these recipes will fit into a single jumbo mug, like the kind you can find at every souvenir shop from Myrtle Beach to Santa Cruz. The golden rule of mug cake baking is to fill the mug no more than half full. If you stick to that, you will avoid overflow (and an extra chore).

Mug cakes don't have to be baked in mugs, but they do need to be baked in something microwavable. Glasses, jars, ceramic ramekins, and even paper cups work well. Keep in mind, however, that they will be hot when they come out of the oven. If there is no handle, a pot holder is useful, and you may want to serve it on a saucer or a plate.

Keep in mind that different containers will require different cooking times. A thin paper cup cooks a mug cake in about a minute. But a thick ceramic mug can take up to 2 minutes. Use your best judgment, and experiment. It only takes one or two mug cakes to become an expert.

MIXING

Some cake recipes have complicated techniques. Not so with mug cakes. Their very nature requires simplicity. With few exceptions, everything is mixed together right in the mug. A fork is the easiest tool to use, and it makes licking the batter practically mandatory.

When recipes call for "mixing" or "stirring" they mean simply that—combining the ingredients loosely. If it requires "beating the batter," that means mix the ingredients completely until they are smooth and lump free. This should take less than a minute. Generally the stirring comes first, and the beating comes at the end. "Folding" means to stir once or twice only, usually to incorporate floating garnishes like chocolate chips or berries. In one or two cases the instruction calls for "whipping," which is a technique designed to incorporate as much air as possible. This is not easy in a mug, and in these cases the recipe will call for a special tool, either a frother, or a whisk and a bowl.

MICROWAVES

There are no special instructions for baking a mug cake. Simply use the basic Cook settings. Just as there are no standard mug sizes, there are also no standard microwaves, but they all work in the same way. Water absorbs the microwave radiation, putting molecules in motion.

The golden brown on the top of traditionally baked cakes is created by the caramelization of sugar, which occurs at 320°F. The temperature in a microwave does not get much hotter than

212°F, the vaporization point of water (because once the water is gone, there is nothing left to heat). As a result, your mug cakes will be, as we say in the business, *blonde*.

The advantage of the microwave oven is, of course, speed. The disadvantage is that such speed makes overcooking a real possibility. The cooking times in this book are given in a range, generally 1½ to 2½ minutes. Always start with the shorter time first. Then check the cake by carefully touching the top. It should be firm and springy, not at all doughy. If necessary, continue cooking in 10 to 15 second increments, until you figure out how long it will take your microwave to cook the cake.

When proteins in the batter start to solidify in a regular oven, the steam and gas generated by the liquids and leavening cause the cake to rise. In the microwave, that rise happens quickly. Once the cakes are removed from the microwave, deflation happens quickly, too. Don't be discouraged by a sinking cake. It is normal. Try to resist the temptation to fill the mug more than half full. If you do, you will likely encounter an overflow problem.

FLOUR

Because the idea behind the mug cake is speed and ease, and because the batches of cake batter are so small, most recipes in the book call for self-rising flour.

DO NOT WORRY IF YOU DO NOT HAVE SELF-RISING FLOUR! (See a substitution ratio on the next page.)

Many mug cakes made with all-purpose flour and a measurement of baking powder or soda often take on a salty, chemical flavor from too much chemical leavening. The self-rising flour solves this problem. In its absence, it is preferable to make your own small batch of self-rising flour, and store it for use in several mug cakes.

But, once you discover how much you love mug cakes, pick up a bag of self-rising flour the next time you are at the market. It will produce better, more consistent mug cakes.

self-rising flour

Recipes for this vary a lot, and include anywhere from ¼ to 1½ teaspoons of baking powder per cup. The following is the most successful, best tasting, best leavening ratio I have found:

INGREDIENTS

1 cup all-purpose flour

¾ teaspoon baking powder

Pinch of kosher salt

METHOD

Whisk the ingredients together with a fork, and store in a dry, airtight container. Measure out from this batch as needed for individual mug cakes.

EGGS ... AND WHY EACH RECIPE MAKES TWO CAKES

To achieve the best consistency and crumb in these cake recipes, it was impossible to make a one-egg cake with the right ratio of ingredients that would fit in a single average mug. And splitting an egg in two is a pain. Therefore, the recipes make enough batter for 2 mugs.

If you want only one cake, you can simply bake it in a giant mug. Otherwise, I suggest you make the recipe as written, then refrigerate or freeze the second mug of batter. It keeps well, and rises fine for another 24 hours. It will freeze for even longer (a couple weeks) if you don't think you'll get another sweet tooth tomorrow. (Yeah, right.) In that case, consider freezing the batter in a paper cup to save space, and keep your coffee mugs in commission. You can bake it frozen, too, right in the paper cup. Just add another 30 seconds or so to the bake time.

Eggs come in several sizes—large, medium, extra large—even jumbo and peewee. All professional bakers use, and refer to, large eggs, and that is exactly what is called for in this book. But (there is always a big but) if all you have in the house is a medium egg, just make the cake anyway. It won't win you a James Beard Award, but it will be a cake, and it will serve its purpose—which is to give you a little extra happy.

If the recipe seems too wet or too dry once it has been mixed, add a touch more water or flour to compensate. That's all there is to it.

DAIRY

Dairy is an important component of cake batter. It adds fat, which increases richness and shelf life; sugars, which aid in caramelization; moisture, which keeps the crumb tender; and flavor, which is yummy.

When a recipe calls for milk it is referring to whole milk, unless otherwise indicated. But that doesn't mean the recipe won't work with 2%, or fat-free milk.

Buttermilk and sour cream are used in traditional baking for their acid content. The acid is necessary to activate leavening in baking soda. But in this book buttermilk and sour cream are used exclusively for flavor. The two are interchangeable and can even be replaced with plain yogurt or milk if necessary. Just keep in mind that the more fat the dairy has, the richer and more tender the finished cake will be.

Cooks should always use unsalted butter, whether they are making mug cakes or roasting a chicken. Unsalted butter lets the butter flavor shine through, and gives the cook control over the salt content.

Some recipes in this book call for cream. In most markets there are several creams to choose from. Whipping cream, which contains about 30 percent fat, and heavy cream, with 35 percent fat, will both work in these recipes. Even light cream, with a measly 18 percent fat, is acceptable. The more fat a cream contains, the better it whips, and the richer the finished dessert will be.

SUGAR

There are two main sugars used in these mug cake recipes—granulated and brown. (There is a discussion of sugar substitutes on pages 98 to 101) Brown and white sugar can be used interchangeably. The flavor will be altered, but the texture and chemistry of the batter will not.

When brown sugar appears in recipes, it means packed brown sugar, unless otherwise specified. (This is true in all books, not just this one.) But if you don't pack your brown sugar, guess what happens? Nothing much. Your cake will just be a little less sweet.

SALT

You will notice that every recipe in this book (with only one or two exceptions) contains salt. Salt is a crucial element in cooking and baking. It is not meant to make stuff taste salty, but to enhance the natural flavors of the other ingredients. It does that by entering the taste buds quickly, opening them up for the other taste elements in the food. Most chefs, including myself, use kosher salt exclusively.

Table salt can be used in these mug cake recipes, but if you have never used kosher salt, consider giving it a try. It is used universally by chefs for its superior flavor, and when your guests see it on your counter, they'll think you're hot stuff.

Fancy salt, like sea salts, marsh salts, fleur de sel, and the like, can be used, but are not necessary. The expense of these salts is wasted in recipes with a multitude of ingredients. Reserve them for dishes that feature the salt, sprinkled over fresh vegetables or meats, or on the top of pastries, as in Caramel Fleur de Sel Mug Cake.

CHOCOLATE

Most chocolate recipes in this book call for chocolate chips. This was done simply for ease of preparation. If you prefer a specific baking chocolate, by all means, use it. Just be sure to cut it into chip-size chunks first. Unless otherwise specified, either semi-sweet or bittersweet chips can be used interchangeably. It is simply a matter of preference. (To the serious chocophiles, one's cocoa percentage preference is a personal and sacred thing.)

When a recipe calls for cocoa powder, it is referring to unsweetened ground cocoa solids. The absence of sugar is the only criteria. Dutch process, ebony, black—any type of unsweetened cocoa powder is fine. But, if all you have is a sweetened cocoa powder, go ahead and use it. Just be sure to reduce the sugar in the recipe. Then put unsweetened cocoa powder on your shopping list.

VANILLA

Certainly the most common pastry flavoring, vanilla is used mainly in extract form. It is made from the seed pods of a tropical orchid. The beans contain thousands of tiny black seeds that carry the flavorful oil. To use a bean in place of extract, slice it lengthwise, scrape out the seeds, and add them to the recipe. The tiny black specs of vanilla seed will indicate that real vanilla was used, and that you are a class act.

When buying extract, avoid imitation vanilla. Vanilla is not the only extract out there, but it is the best. Most of the others have a distinctly artificial flavor. Be aware of the strength of your extracts, and always add just a drop in the beginning. It's easy to add, but impossible to remove.

NUTS

Nuts are a staple ingredient in the bake shop. They can be folded into batters, used as topping, or ground into butter for use as a fatty ingredient. They are loaded with oil, which can be a problem if you don't use them up fast enough. If you are only an occasional nut user, store them in the freezer to prevent rancidity.

Nuts always taste best when toasted, but the task often takes more time than the typical mug-cake baker is willing to spend. If you are up to the challenge, toast a bunch of nuts ahead of time, and keep them in the freezer for impromptu mug caking.

how to toast nuts

Nut toasting is best done in an oven. You may have seen it done on the stovetop, but that is an inferior method. Pan toasting only toasts the part of the nut that touches the pan, so the finished product is spotty brown with an uneven flavor. To do it properly, spread them out on a baking sheet and roast at 350°F for 5 to 10 minutes until their aroma fills the kitchen. Cool toasted nuts completely before grinding or adding them into a recipe. This method also works great for toasting shredded coconut.

2

classics

If you've never made a mug cake before, this is a great place to start. These recipes are the basics, they have simple Ingredients that you probably already have in your kitchen, and they are good recipes to use while testing your microwave's cooking strength and time. After you master one or two, get creative, and use these base recipes to create any number of variations according to your tastes and whims.

As we discussed in the previous section (see page 5), for convenience and ease, most of the recipes in this book are made with self-rising flour. To recap, if you haven't got any on hand, you can make your own self-rising flour by mixing 1 cup of all-purpose flour with ¾ teaspoon of baking powder and a generous pinch of salt. Then measure out as needed for each recipe.

yellow mug cake

Yellow cake is the classic birthday cake, and a perfect blank canvas on which to paint a sweet celebratory picture. Eat it as is, or fold in anything you like—chocolate chips, candies, nuts, fruits—to create a personalized mug cake statement.

INGREDIENTS

2 tablespoons unsalted butter

1 large egg

2 tablespoons milk

1 teaspoon pure vanilla extract

¼ cup granulated sugar

6 tablespoons (¼ cup plus 2 tablespoons) self-rising flour

Pinch of kosher salt

Topping Ideas: Chocolate frosting, vanilla frosting, whipped cream, rainbow sprinkles, chocolate jimmies, or colored sugar crystals.

METHOD

Place the butter in a large mug and microwave it for 20 to 30 seconds until melted. Add the egg and whisk it in with a fork. Stir in the milk, vanilla, and sugar. Add the flour and salt. Beat the batter until smooth. Divide the batter between two mugs. Microwave separately for 1½ to 2½ minutes each until risen and firm.

brown sugar mug cake

MAKES 2 MUG CAKES

The rich molasses flavor of this cake is the perfect starting point for the addition of spices, dried fruits, and nuts. It has a cozy, autumnal flavor, but don't wait until the fall to try it.

INGREDIENTS

1 large egg

2 tablespoons vegetable oil

½ teaspoon pure vanilla extract

½ teaspoon molasses

2 tablespoons milk

¼ cup packed brown sugar

6 tablespoons (¼ cup plus 2 tablespoons) self-rising flour

Pinch of kosher salt

METHOD

In a large mug, whisk together the egg and oil with a fork. Stir in the vanilla, molasses, milk, and brown sugar. Add the flour and salt. Beat the batter until smooth. Divide the batter between two mugs. Microwave separately for 1½ to 2½ minutes each until risen and firm.

Topping Ideas: Penuche fudge frosting, whipped cream, rum-raisin glaze, hard sauce, chopped nuts, raisins, cinnamon-sugar, freshly grated nutmeg, or caramel sauce.

buttermilk mug cake

MAKES 2 MUG CAKES

The tang of buttermilk cuts through the sweetness and gives this batter a distinct flavor that's terrific as is, but also perfectly supports sweet, fruity add-ins like berries and stone fruits.

INGREDIENTS

2 tablespoons unsalted butter

1 large egg

3 tablespoons buttermilk

½ teaspoon pure vanilla extract

¼ cup granulated sugar

6 tablespoons (¼ cup plus 2 tablespoons) self-rising flour

Pinch of kosher salt

METHOD

Place the butter in a large mug and microwave it for 20 to 30 seconds until melted. Add the egg and whisk it in with a fork. Stir in the buttermilk, vanilla, and sugar. Add the flour and salt. Beat the batter until smooth. Divide the batter between two mugs. Microwave separately for 1½ to 2½ minutes each until risen and firm.

Topping Ideas: Sour cream glaze, whipped cream, chocolate ganache, fresh berries, sliced peaches, or chopped pecans.

Variations: The tang of buttermilk can also be achieved using the same amount of sour cream, plain yogurt, or milk with ½ teaspoon of lemon juice or vinegar added.

red velvet mug cake

MAKES 2 MUG CAKES

This über-trendy cake is actually a vintage recipe from the Deep South. It is as red as Scarlet O'Hara's dress thanks to the combination of cocoa powder and cheap liquid red food coloring. Be sure to use the cheap stuff! Fancy food coloring pastes and gels don't work nearly as well. The vinegar was traditionally added to the baking soda as a leavener. With self-rising flour, it's not necessary, but it's added here for its classic zippy flavor.

INGREDIENTS

1 large egg

3 tablespoons vegetable oil

1 teaspoon liquid red food coloring

3 tablespoons buttermilk

2 teaspoons pure vanilla extract

¼ cup granulated sugar

2 tablespoons unsweetened cocoa powder

¼ cup self-rising flour

Pinch of kosher salt

¼ teaspoon cider, white, white wine, or rice vinegar

METHOD

In a large mug, whisk together the egg and oil with a fork. Stir in the food coloring, buttermilk, vanilla, and sugar. Add the cocoa, flour, salt, and vinegar. Beat the batter until smooth. Divide the batter between two mugs. Microwave separately for 1½ to 2½ minutes each until risen and firm.

Topping Ideas: Cream cheese frosting, Marshmallow Fluff, whipped cream, fresh berries, red sugar sprinkles, candied pecans, or chocolate shavings.

Variations

BLUE VELVET: You never know when you may need to make a blue cake. It's easily done by replacing cheap red liquid food coloring with cheap blue liquid food coloring. For any other cake color, you'll want to omit the cocoa powder, as it will give all other food colors a tinge of brown. If you make another color, replace the cocoa powder with an equal amount of flour.

banana mug cake

Overripe bananas are the best choice for baking. Their starch has completely converted to sugar and their soft, mushy texture makes them easy to incorporate into a batter. When your bananas get too ripe to eat out of hand, peel and freeze them in ziplock bags for future mug cakes.

INGREDIENTS

½ overripe banana

1 large egg

1 tablespoon vegetable oil

2 tablespoons buttermilk

½ teaspoon pure vanilla extract

¼ cup packed brown sugar

1 tablespoon chopped walnuts (optional)

½ cup self-rising flour

Pinch of ground cinnamon

Pinch of freshly grated nutmeg

Pinch of kosher salt

METHOD

Place the banana in a mug and mash it well with a fork. Whisk in the egg and oil. Stir in the buttermilk, vanilla, sugar, and nuts. Add the flour, spices, and salt. Beat the batter until smooth. Divide the batter between two mugs. Microwave separately for 1½ to 2½ minutes each until risen and firm.

Topping Ideas: Whipped cream, chocolate ganache, peanut butter frosting, chopped walnuts, shaved chocolate, toasted coconut, cinnamon-sugar, caramel sauce, or shaved chocolate.

Variations: This recipe can be made using any thick fruit or vegetable puree. Try it with sweet potatoes, acorn squash, or apple butter.

strawberry shortmug cake

MAKES 2 MUG CAKES

Shortcake is an American classic. Originally conceived as a way to use up leftover biscuits, it has since evolved into a cake all its own. Don't limit yourself to strawberries! Any fresh seasonal fruit works, as do dried fruits plumped in warm water or liqueur.

INGREDIENTS

Fruit Topping

5 to 6 strawberries, hulled and sliced

Finely grated zest of
1 lemon

1 teaspoon granulated sugar

Mug Cake

1 large egg

½ teaspoon pure vanilla extract

3 tablespoons buttermilk

¼ cup granulated sugar

¼ cup self-rising flour

Pinch of kosher salt

½ cup whipped cream
(page 146)

METHOD

In a small bowl, combine the sliced strawberries, lemon zest, and sugar. Toss them together and set the topping aside to macerate at room temperature while you prepare the cake.

In a large mug, whisk together the egg and vanilla with a fork. Stir in the buttermilk and sugar. Add the flour and salt. Beat the batter until smooth. Divide the batter between two mugs. Microwave separately for 1½ to 2½ minutes each until risen and firm. Top the cakes with the reserved strawberries and the whipped cream.

Variations: Flavor the cake element of this shortcake with chopped nuts, spices, or more citrus zest. Simply fold them into the finished batter before baking.

carrot mug cake

MAKES 2 MUG CAKES

Moist and fruity, this classic has the added bonus of vegetables—to ease your guilt and improve your eyesight.

INGREDIENTS

1 large egg

2 tablespoons vegetable oil

2 tablespoons brown sugar

¼ teaspoon pure vanilla extract

Finely grated zest and juice of 1 small orange (about 2 tablespoons)

¼ cup crushed pineapple, drained

¼ cup grated carrot (about 1 medium carrot)

6 tablespoons (¼ cup plus 2 tablespoons) self-rising flour

Pinch of ground cinnamon

Pinch of freshly grated nutmeg

Pinch of kosher salt

1 tablespoon chopped nuts and/or plumped raisins (optional)

METHOD

In a large mug, whisk together the egg, oil, sugar, vanilla, orange zest, and orange juice with a fork. Stir in the pineapple and grated carrot. Add the flour, spices, and salt. Beat the batter until smooth. Fold in the nuts and raisins. Divide the batter between two mugs. Microwave separately for 1½ to 2½ minutes each until risen and firm.

Topping Ideas: Cream cheese frosting, whipped cream, hard sauce, sour cream glaze, caramel sauce, candied carrot strips, chopped nuts, freshly grated nutmeg or cinnamon-sugar.

oatmeal-raisin mug cake

MAKES 2 MUG CAKES

Oats add a nutty, wholesome flavor and a hearty texture, not to mention added fiber that lowers bad cholesterol and boosts the immune system. Can you think of a better reason to make a mug cake?

INGREDIENTS

3 tablespoons raisins

2 tablespoons apple juice (or rum or brandy)

½ teaspoon pure vanilla extract

1 large egg

3 tablespoons milk

¼ cup packed brown sugar

¼ cup self-rising flour

2 tablespoons oatmeal (old-fashioned oats are preferable to the quick-cooking variety)

Pinch of ground cinnamon

Pinch of kosher

¼ cup streusel (page 157) or 2 tablespoons cinnamon-sugar

METHOD

In a large mug, combine the raisins, apple juice, and vanilla. Microwave for 30 seconds. Set them aside for 5 to 10 minutes to allow the raisins to plump while you make the cake batter.

In a second mug, whisk the egg with a fork. Stir in the milk and brown sugar. Add the flour, oats, cinnamon, and salt. Beat the batter until smooth. Fold in the plumped raisins and juice. Divide the batter between two mugs and top each with streusel or cinnamon-sugar. Microwave separately for 1½ to 2½ minutes each until risen and firm.

Variation: For added texture, replace the oats with prepared granola. The cakes will be a little sweeter and a little crunchier.

Note: Steel-cut oats do not work in this reape unless they are cooked first. Luckily, the cooking is easily done in the microwave. Combine 2 tablespoons of steel-cut oats with 1 tablespoon of water and microwave for 30 seconds. Then add to the recipe as directed.

3

fancy-
schmancy

Sometimes an occasion calls for some sophistication. (Yes, it is possible to create sophistication in a microwave.) Maybe you're trying to impress the cute neighbor across the hall, or you're settling in for a long evening of elegant television viewing. (Dressed in your black-tie Snuggie perhaps?) Such occasions call for more than plain yellow cake. Boredom and a hankerin' for something special are all the excuses you need to try the recipes in this chapter. The techniques are no different, but the ingredients and flavor combinations are something special.

victorian rose mug cake

MAKES 2 MUG CAKES

Rose water was first brought to Victorian England from colonial India, and quickly became all the rage. Enterprising American housewives even distilled their own! Look for it in any Indian or Middle Eastern market.

INGREDIENTS

2 tablespoons unsalted butter, softened

¼ cup granulated sugar

2 teaspoons rose water

1 large egg

2 tablespoons milk

6 tablespoons (¼ cup plus 2 tablespoons) self-rising flour

Pinch of kosher salt

METHOD

In a large mug beat together the butter and sugar with a fork until smooth. Stir in the rose water, egg, and milk. Add the flour and salt. Beat the batter until smooth. Divide the batter between two mugs. Microwave separately for 1½ to 2½ minutes each until risen and firm.

Topping Ideas: Whipped cream, crème fraîche, sour cream frosting, honey glaze, confectioners' sugar, chopped pistachio nuts, fresh berries, dried edible rosebuds or candied rose petals (see recipe below).

Variation: Try replacing the rose water with orange flower water (a common cocktail ingredient, available at liquor stores), or omit it altogether and fold in crushed edible lavender buds for a delicate essence of flowers.

HOW TO MAKE CANDIED ROSE PETALS

To candy rose petals, first make sure they are edible and not covered in pesticides. Coat the separated petals lightly with egg white, then sprinkle with granulated sugar. Set them aside to dry for 5 to 10 minutes before serving.

apple-rosemary mug cake

MAKES 2 MUG CAKES

This might sound unusual, but herbs have long been popular with pastry chefs. Rosemary's distinctive woody, pine-sage aroma is usually paired with stronger flavors that won't be overpowered. But with a light touch, rosemary can beautifully perfume sweet dishes, too.

INGREDIENTS

2 tablespoons unsalted butter

1 teaspoon ground rosemary or fresh, chopped, very fine, or powdered dried rosemary

1 unpeeled apple, grated, any variety (see Note)

1 large egg

2 tablespoons milk

1 teaspoon pure vanilla extract

¼ cup granulated sugar

6 tablespoons (¼ cup plus 2 tablespoons) self-rising flour

Pinch of kosher salt

METHOD

In a large mug, combine the butter, rosemary, and grated apple. Microwave for 1 minute until the butter is melted and the apple is softened. Whisk in the egg with a fork. Stir in the milk, vanilla, and sugar. Add the flour and salt. Beat the batter until smooth. Divide the batter between two mugs. Microwave separately for 1½ to 2½ minutes each until risen and firm.

Topping Ideas: Whipped cream, crème fraîche, chopped almonds, or caramel sauce.

Variation: Rosemary is also lovely with lemon and orange. To make quick work of pulverizing fresh rosemary, use an electric coffee grinder. Be sure to wipe it out when you're through, or your coffee will taste weird. Also try adding it to the Orange Dreamsicle Mug Cake (page 36).

Note: To grate the apple, grate, it skin and all, through the large holes of a box grater. Grate on four sides, stopping short at the core.

caramel–fleur de sel mug cake

MAKES 2 MUG CAKES

This salty-sweet phenomenon is well established, and salted caramels are now everywhere. Fleur de sel is a fancy sea salt, hand harvested from evaporating pools along the coast of Brittany in France. Similar "gourmet" salts can be found from just about everywhere on the planet, and they are definitely worth a few taste tests. You may discover something wonderful! If you don't have sea salt caramel candies on hand, it's fine to use generic caramel candies.

INGREDIENTS

2 tablespoons unsalted butter, softened

¼ cup granulated sugar

1 large egg

½ teaspoon pure vanilla extract

1 tablespoon caramel sauce store-bought or homemade (page 152)

2 tablespoons milk

6 tablespoons (¼ cup plus 2 tablespoons) self-rising flour

½ teaspoon fleur de sel

4 caramel candies, preferably salted

METHOD

In a large mug, whisk together the butter and sugar with a fork. Stir in the egg, vanilla, caramel sauce, and milk. Add the flour and ¼ teaspoon of the fleur de sel. Beat the batter until smooth. Divide the batter between two mugs. Top each mug with a pinch of the remaining fleur de sel. Microwave separately for 30 seconds each. Place two caramel candies on the top of each partially cooked mug cake, then continue cooking 1 to 1½ minutes more until risen and firm.

Topping Ideas: Crème fraîche, fresh peaches, salted peanuts, chopped pecans, or a drizzle of vinegar-caramel sauce.

Variation: Try this recipe using *cajeta*, the Mexican caramel made with goat's milk. Its unique flavor will hook you.

sticky toffee mug cake

MAKES 2 MUG CAKES

From the Lakelands of northern England comes this brilliant half-pudding, half-cake dessert that is as much a part of their heritage as apple pie is to Americans. I'm sure those striving to preserve Lakeland's cultural heritage will cringe at a microwave version of their beloved dessert, but at least we are celebrating it. My apologies, and please pass the forks.

INGREDIENTS

Cake

¼ cup pitted and chopped Medjool dates

¼ cup water

½ teaspoon pure vanilla extract

2 tablespoons unsalted butter

¼ cup granulated sugar

1 large egg

6 tablespoons (¼ cup plus 2 tablespoons) self-rising flour

Pinch of kosher salt

Topping

2 tablespoons brown sugar

2 teaspoons unsalted butter

2 tablespoons heavy cream

METHOD

In a large mug, combine the dates, water, and vanilla. Microwave for 30 seconds, then set aside for 10 minutes to allow the dates to plump.

In a second mug, whisk together the butter and sugar with a fork. Stir in the egg. Add the flour and salt. Beat the batter until smooth. Fold in the plumped dates. Divide the batter between two mugs.

Divide the topping ingredients in half, placing 1 tablespoon of the brown sugar on top of each batter-filled mug, followed by 1 teaspoon of the butter and 1 tablespoon of the cream. Microwave separately for 1 to 2 minutes each until the topping is bubbly and the cake is firm.

Topping Ideas: Whipped cream, crème fraîche, hard sauce, vanilla ice cream, penuche frosting, or caramel sauce.

lemon-thyme mug cake

There is such a plant as lemon thyme, but this recipe refers to the combination of fresh lemon zest and chopped fresh thyme leaves. The result is a sweet and sunny flavor combination you'll use over and over again.

INGREDIENTS

2 tablespoons unsalted butter

Finely grated zest of 1 lemon

1 teaspoon fresh thyme, chopped (or ½ teaspoon dried thyme)

1 large egg

2 tablespoons milk

1 teaspoon pure vanilla extract

¼ cup granulated sugar

6 tablespoons (¼ cup plus 2 tablespoons) self-rising flour

Pinch of kosher salt

METHOD

Place the butter, lemon zest, and thyme in a mug and microwave for 20 seconds until the butter is melted. Whisk in the egg with a fork. Stir in the milk, vanilla, and sugar. Add the flour and salt. Beat the batter until smooth. Divide the batter between two mugs. Microwave separately for 1½ to 2½ minutes each until risen and firm.

Topping Ideas: Whipped cream, lemon curd, equal parts whipped cream and lemon curd folded together, candied lemon zest, sliced almonds, or fresh berries.

Variation: Add ground, freshly toasted anise seeds to the zest and thyme mixture for a delicious, Catalan-inspired taste. (See page 9.)

green tea mug cake

MAKES 2 MUG CAKES

Matcha (or maccha) is the finely powdered green tea used in Japan's cherished tea ceremony. It is also commonly used as a flavoring in a number of food preparations, including noodles, ice cream, and confectionary. The tea is bitter, and during the tea ceremony it is consumed with a small *wagashi* sweet. Here, the effect is simulated by turning the tea itself into a sweet.

INGREDIENTS

1 large egg

2 tablespoons vegetable oil

1 teaspoon matcha powder

2 tablespoons milk

½ teaspoon pure vanilla extract

¼ cup granulated sugar

6 tablespoons (¼ cup plus 2 tablespoons) self-rising flour

Pinch of kosher salt

Note: Instant tea powder is milder than matcha, and often presweetened. You may use it in place of the matcha in this recipe, but reduce the granulated sugar to 2 tablespoons.

METHOD

In a large mug, whisk together the egg, oil, and matcha with a fork. Stir in the milk, vanilla, and sugar. Add the flour and salt. Beat the batter until smooth. Divide the batter between two mugs. Microwave separately for 1½ to 2½ minutes each until risen and firm.

chocolate-pasilla chile mug cake

MAKES 2 MUG CAKES

The chocolate and chile combination has an ancient and noble history. The Aztecs combined them in Xocoatl, and the resulting warrior's drink was coveted, and eventually pinched, by the conquistadors. If you don't have any chile paste lying around, try another hot sauce. Chipotle paste is smokier, while sriracha and Tabasco sauces offer a more acidic effect.

INGREDIENTS

1 large egg

3½ tablespoons vegetable oil

3½ tablespoons milk

¼ teaspoon pure vanilla extract

1 to 3 teaspoons pasilla chile paste

¼ cup packed brown sugar

¼ cup self-rising flour

2 tablespoons unsweetened cocoa powder

Pinch of kosher salt

Topping Ideas: Whipped cream, crème fraîche, chocolate cinnamon sticks, cajeta caramel, or a sprinkle of cinnamon.

METHOD

In a large mug, whisk together the egg and oil with a fork. Stir in the milk, vanilla, chile paste, and brown sugar. Add the flour, cocoa, and salt. Beat the batter until smooth. Divide the batter between two mugs. Microwave separately for 1½ to 2½ minutes each until risen and firm.

HOW TO MAKE YOUR OWN PASILLA CHILE PASTE

To make your own chile paste, toast dried pasilla chile pods briefly in an oven, or in a dry skillet on the stovetop, until just soft to the touch. Let them cool, then remove their stems and seeds. Cover them with hot water and set them aside to macerate for 30 minutes. Drain, reserving the water, then puree the chiles in a food processor or blender, adding back the liquid as necessary. (Reserve the remaining liquid to make rice for your next taco night.)

4

kids' stuff

everyone has a touch of the juvenile, and these recipes will bring that giggly side out every time. If you're "kid-o-phobic," fear not. There needn't be a child within miles to try these mugs. But be warned— if there are tots lurking about, you may need to fight them off.

This chapter contains, not surprisingly, a fair amount of marshmallows. It bears mentioning that marshmallows expand tremendously in the microwave. To that end, the recipes have been adjusted accordingly. Marshmallow Fluff can be tamed when swirled into a batter. Mini marshmallows are restrained when the batter contains other chunky Ingredients. Large marshmallows are avoided completely, as they cause an eruption to rival Vesuvius. However, if you're the type to improvise, or add a little extra (which I applaud), be sure to choose a mug big enough to accommodate the expansion.

moon pie mug cake

MAKES 2 MUG CAKES

If you've never had a Moon Pie, you haven't lived. If you have, you will be happy to discover that its wonderment is easily replicated in a mug. Created in 1917 as a portable lunch dessert for Tennessee coal miners, the Moon Pie caught on quick. In the 1950s, a Moon Pie and an RC Cola could be had for a dime, and the two are now an inseparable Southern snack institution.

INGREDIENTS

1 large egg

3½ tablespoons vegetable oil

3½ tablespoons milk

¼ cup granulated sugar

¼ teaspoon pure vanilla extract

2 tablespoons unsweetened cocoa powder

¼ cup self-rising flour

Pinch of kosher salt

2 graham crackers, broken into small pieces

¼ cup mini marshmallows, or Marshmallow Fluff

2 tablespoons chocolate chips

Topping Ideas: Whipped cream sweetened with RC Cola, Marshmallow Fluff, crumbled graham crackers, or chocolate jimmies.

METHOD

In a large mug, whisk together the egg and oil with a fork. Stir in the milk, sugar, vanilla, and cocoa. Add the flour and salt. Beat the batter until smooth. Fold in the graham cracker bits, marshmallows, and chocolate chips. Divide the batter between two mugs. Microwave separately for 1½ to 2½ minutes each until risen and firm.

fluffernutter mug cake

MAKES 2 MUG CAKES

Marshmallow Fluff is a Massachusetts invention, and is not readily available outside of New England. The rest of the country must make do with Marshmallow Creme. The fluffernutter sandwich comes from Massachusetts, too. Several attempts at making it the state sandwich have failed, probably due to health concerns. Maybe they should try it on whole wheat bread.

INGREDIENTS

2 tablespoons peanut butter

1 large egg

1 tablespoon vegetable oil

¼ cup milk

¼ teaspoon pure vanilla extract

¼ cup packed brown sugar

5 tablespoons (¼ cup plus 1 tablespoon) self-rising flour

Pinch of kosher salt

2 tablespoons Marshmallow Fluff or Marshmallow Creme

METHOD

In a large mug, whisk together the peanut butter, egg, and oil with a fork. Stir in the milk, vanilla, and brown sugar. Add the flour and salt. Beat the batter until smooth. Fold in the marshmallow fluff. Divide the batter between two mugs. Microwave separately for 1½ to 2½ minutes each until risen and firm.

Topping Ideas: Whipped cream, another dollop of fluff (if you dare), sliced bananas, chopped peanuts, chocolate sauce, or chocolate shavings.

Variations

NUTELLA-FLUFFER: Replace the peanut butter with Nutella.

FLUFFER-NANA-NUTTER: Fold sliced ripe bananas into the batter.

PORKY-NUTTER: Fold crumbled bacon into the batter.

orange dreamsicle
mug cake

MAKES 2 MUG CAKES

A classic sidewalk sundae, the dreamsicle's iconic combination of vanilla and orange is the epitome of summer, with a flavor reminiscent of running around barefoot on the too-hot sidewalk. They come in other flavors, too, but orange is the bomb.

INGREDIENTS

1 large egg

3 tablespoons vegetable oil

Finely grated zest of half an orange (or ⅛ teaspoon orange extract)

2 tablespoons fresh orange juice

¼ cup granulated sugar

6 tablespoons (¼ cup plus 2 tablespoons) self-rising flour

Pinch of kosher salt

¼ cup mini marshmallows

METHOD

In a large mug, whisk together the egg and oil with a fork. Stir in the zest, juice, and sugar. Add the flour and salt. Beat the batter until smooth. Fold in the marshmallows. Divide the batter between two mugs. Microwave separately for 1½ to 2½ minutes each until risen and firm.

Topping Ideas: Whipped cream, chocolate fudge frosting, chocolate ganache, orange glaze, grated chocolate, candied orange zest, or Marshmallow Fluff.

pb and j mug cake

This is certainly the most American of flavor pairs. Whether you lean toward chunky or smooth, grape jelly or strawberry jam, the flavor of this mug will remind you of the lunchroom at your grammar school, minus the "Lunch Lady."

INGREDIENTS

2 tablespoons peanut butter

1 large egg

1 tablespoon vegetable oil

¼ cup milk

¼ teaspoon pure vanilla extract

¼ cup packed brown sugar

⅓ cup self-rising flour

Pinch of kosher salt

2 tablespoons favorite jam or jelly

Topping Ideas: Sweetened whipped cream, banana slices, fresh berries, or chopped peanuts.

METHOD

In a large mug, whisk together the peanut butter and egg with a fork. Stir in the oil, milk, vanilla, and sugar. Add the flour and salt. Beat the batter until smooth. Divide the batter between two mugs. Top each with a generous tablespoon of jelly. Microwave separately for 1½ to 2½ minutes each until risen and firm.

Variations: Omit the jelly and fold in your favorite peanut butter partner such as banana, raisins, honey (peanut butter and honey are collectively known as "peanut-bunny"), bacon bits, or potato chips.

root beer float mug cake

MAKES 2 MUG CAKES

Traditionally brewed from sarsaparilla or sassafras roots, today's root beer is an amalgam of dozens of flavors, including vanilla, cinnamon, nutmeg, molasses, licorice, fenugreek, and hops. For authenticity, top this one with a scoop of vanilla ice cream.

INGREDIENTS

2 tablespoons unsalted butter, softened

1 tablespoon brown sugar

2 tablespoons granulated sugar

1 large egg

3 tablespoons root beer

¼ teaspoon root beer extract or pure vanilla extract

6 tablespoons (¼ cup plus 2 tablespoons) self-rising flour

Pinch of kosher salt

Topping Ideas: Vanilla ice cream, whipped cream, or Marshmallow Fluff.

METHOD

In a large mug, whisk together the butter and sugars with a fork. Stir in the egg, root beer, and extract. Add the flour and salt. Beat the batter until smooth. Divide the batter between two mugs. Microwave separately for 1½ to 2½ minutes each until risen and firm.

Note: Root beer extract will really pump up the flavor of this cake. Larger supermarkets or confectionary stores often carry it, or it can be found online.

s'mores mug cake

MAKES 2 MUG CAKES

Nostalgia for the s'more got out of hand a decade ago when high-end pastry chefs started making their own marshmallows and graham crackers, and serving it all with little sticks and Bunsen burners for table-top roasting. I say if you aren't covered with campsite dust, it's not really a s'more. That said, sometimes the essence of camp is just what the doctor ordered.

INGREDIENTS

2 tablespoons unsalted butter

1 large egg

2 tablespoons milk

1 teaspoon pure vanilla extract

¼ cup granulated sugar

6 tablespoons (¼ cup plus 2 tablespoons) self-rising flour

Pinch of kosher salt

1 graham cracker, broken into small pieces

2 tablespoons chocolate chips

2 tablespoons mini marshmallows

METHOD

Place the butter in a large mug and microwave for 20 to 30 seconds until melted. Whisk in the egg with a fork. Stir in the milk, vanilla, and sugar. Add the flour and salt. Beat the batter until smooth. Fold in the graham cracker pieces, chocolate chips, and marshmallows. Divide the batter between two mugs. Microwave separately for 1½ to 2½ minutes each until risen and firm.

Topping Ideas: Eat this as is. It's hard to improve perfection. (However, a sprinkle of campfire ashes, though inedible, would make it more authentic.)

sno-ball mug cake

MAKES 2 MUG CAKES

If you don't know what a Sno-Ball is, you should probably move on to the next chapter. Those round, fuzzy pink flavor wads are a staple of childhood (and a guilty pleasure of adulthood). Food coloring is optional here, but without it, this recipe looks much too grown-up.

INGREDIENTS

1 large egg

3 tablespoons milk

¼ teaspoon pure vanilla extract

¼ teaspoon coconut extract

1 drop pink liquid food coloring

¼ cup granulated sugar

⅓ cup self-rising flour

Pinch of kosher salt

¼ cup Marshmallow Fluff or mini marshmallows

Sweetened Whipped Cream (page 146)

¼ cup shredded coconut (sweetened or unsweetened are both fine)

METHOD

In a large mug, whisk together the egg and milk with a fork. Stir in the extracts, food coloring, and sugar. Add the flour and salt. Beat the batter until smooth. Swirl in the Marshmallow fluff. Divide the batter between two mugs. Microwave separately for 1½ to 2½ minutes each until risen and firm. Top each with a dollop of the whipped cream and shredded coconut.

Note: To color your coconut pink, combine a handful of coconut and a drop of liquid food coloring in a ziplock bag, then knead it to spread the color. (Paste or gel food coloring doesn't work well here, as they tend to clump.)

5

adults only

Sometimes, after a long day, you need time to yourself, away from the kids, so you can microwave in peace. So when those little cherubs finally go to sleep, it's party time. The alcohol content of these cakes is negligible, and it certainly won't intoxicate. Still, there's no reason to waste good booze on the kids.

amaretto mug cake

MAKES 2 MUG CAKES

This Italian liqueur's distinct bitter-almond flavor comes not from bitter almonds, but from the pits of apricots. The two trees are both of the genus *Prunus* (as are the other stone fruits), so the flavor similarity is not too surprising. In this recipe, the amaretti macaroons can be left out if you're not lucky enough to have some on hand, but they do add a stellar touch.

INGREDIENTS

1 large egg

3 tablespoons vegetable oil

3 tablespoons amaretto

¼ cup granulated sugar

2 tablespoons crushed sliced almonds, toasted if possible

6 tablespoons (¼ cup plus 2 tablespoons) self-rising flour

Pinch of kosher salt

2 amaretti macaroons, crushed (reserve a little for garnish)

METHOD

In a large mug, whisk together the egg and oil with a fork. Stir in the amaretto, sugar, and almonds. Add the flour and salt. Beat the batter until smooth. Fold in macaroons. Divide the batter between two mugs. Microwave separately for 1½ to 2½ minutes each until risen and firm.

Topping Ideas: Whipped cream spiked with amaretto or toasted sliced almonds.

Variation: Bake each mug with a generous topping of streusel that has been enhanced with a few chopped almonds.

Note: If you'd like to avoid the alcohol, you can make this using almond extract, but be careful! A little almond extract goes a long, long way. Use only a drop.

piña colada mug cake

MAKES 2 MUG CAKES

The official drink of Puerto Rico, the piña colada gained popularity on the mainland in the 1950s. Creation of the drink is claimed by several hotels and bars and a seventeenth-century pirate.

INGREDIENTS

1 large egg

3 tablespoons rum

3 tablespoons crushed pineapple, drained, juice reserved

¼ teaspoon pure vanilla extract

¼ teaspoon coconut extract

¼ cup granulated sugar

⅓ cup self-rising flour

Pinch of kosher salt

¼ cup shredded coconut (sweetened or unsweetened are both fine)

Topping Ideas: Rum glaze, grilled pineapple sauce, shredded toasted coconut, a skewer of tropical fruit, or a tiny umbrella.

METHOD

In a large mug, whisk together the egg and 2 tablespoons rum with a fork. Stir in the pineapple extracts and sugar. Add the flour, salt, and coconut. Beat the batter until smooth. Divide the batter between two mugs. Microwave separately for 1½ to 2½ minutes each until risen and firm.

Combine the reserved pineapple juice with the remaining 1 tablespoon rum and drizzle over the cakes when they come out of the microwave.

irish coffee mug cake

MAKES 2 MUG CAKES

This drink supposedly originated at the Shannon County Airport in Ireland, but its popularity in the States can be traced to San Francisco's Buena Vista Café. While there are those who'll dispute its origin, the Buena Vista is the place to go to warm your insides on a foggy night by The Bay.

INGREDIENTS

1 large egg

3 tablespoons vegetable oil

1 tablespoon sour cream

1 tablespoon espresso powder (or instant coffee)

3 tablespoons good-quality Irish whiskey

¼ cup granulated sugar

5 tablespoons self-rising flour

Pinch of kosher salt

½ cup Sweetened Whipped Cream (page 146)

METHOD

In a large mug, whisk together the egg and oil with a fork. Stir in the sour cream, espresso powder, whiskey, and sugar. Add the flour and salt. Beat the batter until smooth. Divide the batter between two mugs. Microwave separately for 1½ to 2½ minutes each until risen and firm. Top each with a dollop of the sweetened whipped cream.

espresso mug cake

MAKES 2 MUG CAKES

Espresso is a grown-up drink, to be sure, although some kids might benefit from a jolt of caffeine in the morning. The key to this rich cake is good-quality espresso powder or extract. Luckily, Starbucks now makes a decent instant coffee, which does the trick nicely.

INGREDIENTS

1 large egg

3 tablespoons vegetable oil

1 teaspoon espresso powder (or instant coffee)

3 tablespoons milk

3 tablespoons granulated sugar

⅓ cup self-rising flour

Pinch of kosher salt

METHOD

In a large mug, whisk together the egg and oil with a fork. Stir in the espresso powder, milk, and sugar. Add the flour and salt. Beat the batter until smooth. Divide the batter between two mugs. Microwave separately for 1½ to 2½ minutes each until risen and firm.

Topping Ideas: Whipped cream, caramel cream, chocolate shavings, chocolate sauce, caramel sauce, or a dash of ground cinnamon.

Variations

CARAMEL MACCHIATO: Fold 2 tablespoons of caramel sauce into the batter before cooking.

CINNAMON AMERICANO: Add ¼ teaspoon of cinnamon with the flour.

HAZELNUT LATTE: Fold in ¼ cup of chopped hazelnuts to the batter before cooking.

TURKISH COFFEE: Double the espresso powder and add ½ teaspoon of ground cardamom.

better-than-sex mug cake

MAKES 2 MUG CAKES

The only reason this recipe appears in this chapter is because of the title. If you want to serve it to kids, knock yourself out...although you might want to rename it "Better-than-Bieber" cake.

INGREDIENTS

1 large egg

3½ tablespoons vegetable oil

3½ tablespoons sweetened condensed milk

2 tablespoons unsweetened cocoa powder

1 tablespoon brown sugar

¼ cup self-rising flour

Pinch of kosher salt

1½ tablespoons caramel sauce, storebought or home-made (page 152)

1 crushed Heath bar (or other favorite candy bar)

METHOD

In a large mug, whisk together the egg and oil with a fork. Stir in the sweetened condensed milk, cocoa, and brown sugar. Add the flour and salt. Beat the batter until smooth. Swirl in the caramel sauce and crushed candy bar. Divide the batter between two mugs. Microwave separately for 1½ to 2½ minutes each until risen and firm.

Topping Ideas: Whipped cream, candied nuts, caramel sauce, chocolate fudge icing, chopped nuts, chocolate shavings, or more candy bar bits.

Note: The sweetened condensed milk adds the extreme decadence that gives this cake its name. If you don't have any on hand, plain milk is fine. If such substitutions are made, one might, again, consider renaming the cake—perhaps "Better-Than-Holding-Hands Cake."

orange-grand marnier mug cake

MAKES 2 MUG CAKES

There are several orange brandies on the market besides Grand Marnier, including Cointreau and Triple Sec (which is much cheaper). Any of them will yield great results. The grated orange zest gives this cake its punch of orange flavor.

INGREDIENTS

1 large egg

3 tablespoons vegetable oil

Finely Grated zest of ½ orange

3 tablespoons Grand Marnier

¼ cup granulated sugar

6 tablespoons (¼ cup plus 2 tablespoons) self-rising flour

Pinch of kosher salt

METHOD

In a large mug, whisk together the egg and oil with a fork. Stir in the orange zest, Grand Marnier, and sugar. Add the flour and salt. Beat the batter until smooth. Divide the batter between two mugs. Microwave separately for 1½ to 2½ minutes each until risen and firm.

Topping Ideas: Whipped cream, Grand Marnier glaze, crème fraîche, orange slices, shaved chocolate, or candied orange peel.

Note: You can replace the alcohol with an equal amount of milk or orange juice concentrate, and add ⅛ teaspoon of orange extract for similar, nonalcoholic results.

pink champagne mug cake

This mug cake is perfect for Sunday brunch, or when unexpected guests pop in at 11:55 P.M. on January 31. The strawberries add just the right amount of sweetness to balance the acidity of the wine. They also look cute.

INGREDIENTS

4 strawberries, washed, dried, and diced

¼ cup champagne

1 large egg

1 tablespoon unsalted butter, softened

1 drop pink food coloring

¼ cup granulated sugar

6 tablespoons (¼ cup plus 2 tablespoons) self-rising flour

Pinch of kosher salt

Topping Ideas:
Whipped cream, sifted confectioners' sugar, or fresh berries.

METHOD

In a large mug, combine the strawberries and champagne. Set them aside to macerate for 5 to 10 minutes.

In a second mug, whisk together the egg and butter with a fork. Stir in the food coloring, sugar, macerated strawberries, and their liquid. Add the flour and salt. Beat the batter until smooth. Divide the batter between two mugs. Microwave separately for 1½ to 2½ minutes each until risen and firm.

Variations

MIMOSA MUG CAKE: Omit the food coloring and add the finely grated zest of 1 orange, or 1 teaspoon of orange juice concentrate.

BEER MUG CAKE: Omit the food coloring and berries, add ½ teaspoon of vanilla extract, and replace the champagne with your favorite beer.

GUINNESS MUG CAKE: Follow Beer Mug Cake instructions above, and replace 2 tablespoons of flour with unsweetened cocoa powder.

Note: For our photograph, we rolled our strawberry in edible gold powder, which is available at specialty cake decorating supply stores and online.

6

choc-o-rama

every pastry chef knows that no menu is complete without at least one chocolate item. Translated into home-chef speak, you should always be equipped with the basic chocolate ingredients. A ready supply of chocolate chips and cocoa powder lets you whip up a chocolate mug cake at a moment's notice.

devil's food mug cake

MAKES 2 MUG CAKES

The name of this cake comes from the devilishly reddish tinge created when cocoa powder is mixed with baking soda. This effect doesn't work with the self-rising flour, so for this recipe we are using regular all-purpose flour.

INGREDIENTS

1 large egg

3½ tablespoons vegetable oil

3½ tablespoons buttermilk

¼ cup granulated sugar

¼ teaspoon pure vanilla extract

¼ cup all-purpose flour

2 tablespoons unsweetened cocoa powder

⅛ teaspoon baking soda (a generous pinch)

Pinch of kosher salt

METHOD

In a large mug, whisk together the egg and oil with a fork. Stir in the buttermilk, sugar, and vanilla. Add the flour, cocoa, baking soda, and salt. Beat the batter until smooth. Divide the batter between two mugs. Microwave separately for 1½ to 2½ minutes each until risen and firm.

Topping Ideas: Whipped cream, chocolate ganache, vanilla frosting, chocolate sauce, caramel sauce, shaved chocolate, raspberry sauce, or chopped nuts.

Note: If you don't care about the reddish brown color, omit the baking soda and use self-rising flour instead. The flavor is indistinguishable.

mexican chocolate mug cake

MAKES 2 MUG CAKES

Mexican chocolate is a coarse, sweet, cinnamony disk used to make Mexico's traditional hot chocolate, and the savory sauce called *mole*. The flavor is superb, but it is not meant to be eaten out of hand, because the sugar is gritty and undissolved. It is available in most supermarkets and Mexican markets, but if you can't find it, simulate it by adding $\frac{1}{8}$ teaspoon of cinnamon to $\frac{1}{4}$ cup of semisweet chocolate chips.

INGREDIENTS

2 tablespoons unsalted butter

½ wheel Mexican chocolate, chopped

1 large egg

3½ tablespoons milk

¼ teaspoon pure vanilla extract

¼ cup packed brown sugar

2 tablespoons unsweetened cocoa powder

2 tablespoons self-rising flour

Pinch of kosher salt

Topping Ideas: Whipped cream, crema, caramel sauce, *cajeta*, shaved chocolate, a dusting of ground cinnamon, or chopped pecans.

METHOD

Combine the butter and Mexican chocolate in a large mug. Microwave for 30 to 60 seconds until melted. Whisk with a fork to combine, then whisk in the egg. Stir in the milk, vanilla, brown sugar, and cocoa. Add the flour and salt. Beat the batter until smooth. Divide the batter between two mugs. Microwave separately for 1½ to 2½ minutes each until risen and firm.

Note: If you are simulating Mexican chocolate by adding cinnamon to chocolate, be sure to pick the right cinnamon. There are actually two types of bark sold as cinnamon; cassia, which is very hard, and difficult to break or grind, and cinnamon (sometimes called Mexican cinnamon), which is very brittle. Most ground cinnamon sold in the United States comes from cassia bark. But true cinnamon is the one used in Mexican chocolate. It has a spicier flavor, like the "red-hot" candies, and it is readily available in sticks at Mexican markets. It is very easy to pulverize in a coffee grinder or mortar.

black forest mug cake

MAKES 2 MUG CAKES

This classic chocolate-cherry cake was known originally as *schwarzwälder kirschtorte*. It was named for the distilled cherry brandy *kirschwasser*, used to flavor the cake, which hails from the Schwarzwäld (Black Forest) mountain range in southwestern Germany. The brandy's distinct flavor is created by distilling not only the cherry fruit, but also the pits, which lend a nutty essence to the finished product.

INGREDIENTS

¼ cup chopped cherries, canned or fresh

2 tablespoons kirschwasser, brandy, or rum

1 large egg

3 tablespoons vegetable oil

3 tablespoons sour cream

¼ teaspoon pure vanilla extract

¼ cup granulated sugar

2 tablespoons unsweetened cocoa powder

¼ cup self-rising flour

Pinch of kosher salt

½ cup Sweetened Whipped Cream (page 146)

2 tablespoons shaved chocolate

METHOD

In a large mug, combine the cherries and kirsch. Microwave for 20 seconds to warm through. Set aside.

In a second mug, whisk together the egg and oil with a fork. Stir in the sour cream, vanilla, and sugar. Add the cocoa, flour, and salt. Beat the batter until smooth. Fold in the cherries and kirsch. Divide the batter between two mugs. Microwave separately for 1½ to 2½ minutes each until risen and firm.

Top each cake with a dollop of sweetened whipped cream and garnish with shaved chocolate.

chocolate mayonnaise mug cake

MAKES 1 MUG CAKE

Mayonnaise is an all-American cake ingredient, first popularized during World War II when rationing eliminated many items from the baker's pantry, including butter. As a result, mayonnaise companies capitalized on the idea, and began printing mayonnaise cake recipes in booklets and on their labels.

INGREDIENTS

1 tablespoon mayonnaise

3 tablespoons granulated sugar

2 tablespoons water

½ teaspoon pure vanilla extract

1 tablespoon unsweetened cocoa powder

¼ cup self-rising flour

Pinch of kosher salt

METHOD

In a large mug, whisk together the mayonnaise and sugar with a fork. Stir in the water and vanilla. Add the cocoa flour and salt. Beat the batter until smooth. Microwave the cake for 1 to 2 minutes until risen and firm.

Topping Ideas: Whipped cream, chocolate whipped cream, crème fraîche, chocolate sour cream frosting, chopped nuts, shaved chocolate, or fresh fruit.

deep dark chocolate mug cake

MAKES 2 MUG CAKES

This mug cake is rich and moist—more like a brownie than a cake. It is perfect for the truly serious chocoholic. (Although, it's worth noting that there is no such thing as "chocohol.")

INGREDIENTS

2 tablespoons unsalted butter

¼ cup dark chocolate chips (semisweet or bittersweet)

1 large egg

3½ tablespoons buttermilk

¼ teaspoon pure vanilla extract

¼ cup granulated sugar

2 tablespoons unsweetened cocoa powder

2 tablespoons self-rising flour

Pinch of kosher salt

METHOD

Combine the butter and chocolate chips in a large mug. Microwave for 30 to 60 seconds until melted. Add the egg and whisk it in with a fork. Stir in the buttermilk, vanilla, sugar, and cocoa. Add the flour and salt. Beat the batter until smooth. Divide the batter between two mugs. Microwave separately for 1½ to 2½ minutes each until risen and firm.

Topping Ideas: Whipped cream, chocolate whipped cream, crème fraîche, ganache, orange segments, fresh berries, or shaved chocolate.

chocolate turtle mug cake

MAKES 2 MUG CAKES

Caramel and pecans dipped in chocolate got the name "turtle" in the 1920s because of their shape—a round chocolate-covered blob of caramel with pecan halves that stuck out like turtle feet. It's not the most appetizing name, but the flavors are a classic.

INGREDIENTS

1 large egg

3½ tablespoons vegetable oil

3½ tablespoons milk

2 tablespoons granulated sugar

¼ teaspoon pure vanilla extract

2 tablespoons unsweetened cocoa powder

¼ cup self-rising flour

Pinch of kosher salt

2 tablespoons Caramel Sauce store-bought or homemade (page 152)

¼ cup pecan pieces, preferably toasted (See page 9)

METHOD

In a large mug, whisk together the egg and oil with a fork. Stir in the milk, sugar, and vanilla. Add the cocoa, flour, and salt. Beat the batter until smooth. Swirl in the caramel sauce and pecans. Divide the batter between two mugs. Microwave separately for 1½ to 2½ minutes each until risen and firm.

Topping Ideas: Whipped cream, caramel cream, crème fraîche, chopped nuts, chocolate sauce, caramel sauce, vinegar-caramel sauce, salted caramel sauce, or candied pecans.

chocolate-raspberry mug cake

MAKES 2 MUG CAKES

Chocolate and raspberries are a classic pair. The tangy, tart fruit cuts through the rich chocolate for a perfect balance.

INGREDIENTS

2 tablespoons unsalted butter

¼ cup dark chocolate chips (semisweet or bittersweet)

1 large egg

3½ tablespoons milk

¼ teaspoon pure vanilla extract

¼ cup granulated sugar

2 tablespoons unsweetened cocoa powder

2 tablespoons self-rising flour

Pinch of kosher salt

¼ cup fresh or frozen raspberries

Topping Ideas: Whipped cream, chocolate whipped cream, chocolate ganache.

METHOD

Combine the butter and chocolate in a large mug. Microwave for 30 to 60 seconds until melted. Whisk with a fork to combine, then whisk in the egg. Stir in the milk, vanilla, sugar, and cocoa. Add the flour and salt. Beat the batter until smooth. Fold in the raspberries. Divide the batter between two mugs. Microwave separately for 1½ to 2½ minutes each until risen and firm.

white chocolate mug cake

This basic white batter uses buttermilk to cut through the richness, and highlight the vanilla. Sour cream and plain yogurt have the same effect, so feel free to experiment with the dairy portion of this recipe.

INGREDIENTS

2 tablespoons unsalted butter

¼ cup white chocolate chips

1 large egg

3½ tablespoons buttermilk

¼ teaspoon pure vanilla extract

2 tablespoons granulated sugar

5 tablespoons (¼ cup plus 1 tablespoon) self-rising flour

Pinch of kosher salt

METHOD

Combine the butter and white chocolate chips in a large mug. Microwave them for 20 to 40 seconds until melted. Whisk with a fork to combine, then whisk in the egg. Stir in the buttermilk, vanilla, and sugar. Add the flour and salt. Beat the batter until smooth. Divide the batter between two mugs. Microwave separately for 1½ to 2½ minutes each until risen and firm.

Topping Ideas: Crème fraîche, whipped cream, vinegar-caramel sauce, espresso chocolate sauce, fruit sauce, fresh berries, orange, or grapefruit supremes (page 67).

Variation: To enhance the acidity, replace the sugar with 2 tablespoons honey. Honey is sweeter than granulated sugar, but it also has a little acidic bite.

7

a little fruity

fruit is nature's dessert. Sweet and crisp or warm and steamy, fruit is a must on every dessert menu, and it's the healthiest way to add flavor and texture to your mugs.

Historically, fruit was a luxury, available only in the warmer months, and preserved through drying, canning, or fermenting and hoarded for special occasions. Plum Pudding, a winter tradition, didn't actually contain plums, but a variety of such dried fruits, all of which were referred to as "plums."

Today, air travel and refrigerated shipping allows us to have any fresh fruit we want, whenever we want it. Whatever it's doing to our planet, it certainly affords us some great dessert options. But if you're concerned about fossil fuels (as you should be), look for locally grown fruits, and pick what's in season. It will make your cakes better, and your conscience clearer.

black cherry mug cake

MAKES 2 MUG CAKES

The dark, bittersweet black cherry has a sharper flavor than lighter sweet cherries like the Bing. Their acidity makes them great for baking, when the addition of sugar to a batter gives just the right balance.

INGREDIENTS

½ cup pitted fresh or canned black cherries (if canned, drain and reserve the syrup)

2 tablespoons unsalted butter

1 large egg

1 tablespoon sour cream

¼ teaspoon pure vanilla extract

¼ cup granulated sugar

2 tablespoons cocoa powder

¼ cup self-rising flour

Pinch of kosher salt

METHOD

Combine the cherries and butter in a large mug. Microwave for 30 seconds until the butter is melted. Whisk in the egg with a fork. Stir in the sour cream, vanilla, and sugar. Add the cocoa, flour and salt. Beat the batter until smooth. Divide the batter between two mugs. Microwave separately for 1½ to 2½ minutes each until risen and firm.

Topping Ideas: Whipped cream, cherry glaze, kirsch-cherry sauce made with reserved cherry syrup, kirsch-flavored hard sauce, shaved chocolate, unsweetened cocoa powder, or confectioners' sugar.

Variations

BLACKBERRY MUG CAKE: Substitute blackberries for cherries, and add a dash of crème de cassis (black currant liqueur) if you've got any on hand.

citrus-bay laurel mug cake

MAKES 2 MUG CAKES

Bay is usually remembered as that annoying leaf your mom always forgets to pull out of the stew. But the piney aroma of the leaf sweetens as it dries, and becomes a lovely accompaniment to fruits. Pulverize dry bay leaves in a coffee mill to create a fine, aromatic powder.

INGREDIENTS

1 large egg

3 tablespoons vegetable oil

½ teaspoon pulverized bay leaves

Finely grated zest of 1 lemon

1 tablespoon fresh orange juice

1 tablespoon fresh lime juice

1 tablespoon milk

¼ cup granulated sugar

6 tablespoons (¼ cup plus 2 tablespoons) self-rising flour

Pinch of kosher salt

¼ cup citrus segments (see instructions)

Topping Ideas: Whipped cream, lemon curd, confectioners' sugar, or candied citrus zest.

METHOD

In a large mug, whisk together the egg, oil, and bay with a fork. Stir in the zest, juices, milk, and sugar. Add the flour and salt. Beat the batter until smooth. Fold in the citrus segments. Divide the batter between two mugs. Microwave separately for 1½ to 2½ minutes each until risen and firm.

Variations: Bay mug cakes taste lovely with berries and stone fruits, too. Increase the milk to 3 tablespoons, omit the zest and juice, and replace the citrus segments with the stone fruit of choice.

HOW TO SEGMENT CITRUS

The *supreme* is the very best part of the citrus. To get it, slice the top and bottom off the citrus fruit so it stands up straight and doesn't roll. With a sharp knife, slice from the top of the fruit to the bottom, removing the rind and the pith all the way around the fruit. The brightly colored inner fruit should be exposed, and every bit of clinging white pith should be removed.

Now, hold the fruit in your hand and slice to the center on each side of each membrane that divides each section. As you do this, the suprêmes should fall out. (They look like naked sections.) A serrated knife works best for this job.

applesauce mug cake

MAKES 1 MUG CAKE

Apples are available all year, but that doesn't mean they are always good. Their true season is in the early fall, when the varieties abound. The rest of the year your choice is pretty much limited to red or green. To get the best, crisp apple-y flavor out of season, reach for a container of applesauce. There are some great ones on the market, and they add not only flavor, but moisture, to your mug.

INGREDIENTS

3 tablespoons applesauce

3 tablespoons maple syrup

½ teaspoon pure vanilla extract

¼ cup self-rising flour

Pinch of ground cinnamon

Punch of kosher salt

METHOD

In a large mug, whisk together the applesauce, maple syrup, and vanilla with a fork. Add the flour, cinnamon, and salt. Beat the batter until smooth. Microwave the cake for 1½ to 2½ minutes until risen and firm.

Topping Ideas: Whipped cream, sour cream, penuche frosting, maple frosting, maple glaze, apple glaze, cinnamon-sugar, or candied walnuts.

Variation: This cake will work similarly with any thick fruit puree. Try it with pureed pear, prune, pumpkin, or sweet potato.

Note: You can spice this cake up with the addition of the typical "pumpkin pie spice," or your own blend of cinnamon, nutmeg, cardamom, cloves, and white pepper.

strawberry-rhubarb mug cake

MAKES 2 MUG CAKES

The rhubarb, also known as pie plant, is technically a vegetable, and looks like fat red celery. Its tart flavor is reminiscent of the cranberry, and like the cranberry it needs a lot of sugar.

INGREDIENTS

¼ cup fresh rhubarb, leaves removed, finely chopped

2 tablespoons unsalted butter

1 large egg

3 tablespoons milk

¼ teaspoon pure vanilla extract

¼ cup granulated sugar

6 tablespoons (¼ cup plus 2 tablespoons) self-rising flour

Pinch of ground cardamom or freshly grated nutmeg

Pinch of kosher salt

3 to 4 fresh strawberries, hulled and finely chopped

METHOD

In a large mug, combine the rhubarb and butter. Microwave for 30 seconds to warm through. Whisk in the egg with a fork. Stir in the milk, vanilla, and sugar. Add the flour, cardamom, and salt. Beat the batter until smooth. Fold in the chopped strawberries. Divide the batter between two mugs. Microwave separately for 1½ to 2½ minutes each until risen and firm.

Topping Ideas: Whipped cream, strawberry cream, strawberry sauce, confectioners' sugar, freshly grated nutmeg, or sliced strawberries.

caramel pear mug cake

MAKES 2 MUG CAKES

Caramel and apples are the classic combination, but the creamy, buttery pear is a fantastic alternative. Fall is pear season, and that's when you'll find the markets full of that soft, sweet fruit. Use any of them except the brown, woody Bosc pear, which is better suited to poaching.

INGREDIENTS

1 ripe pear, grated or diced

3 tablespoons vegetable oil

1 large egg

3½ tablespoons milk

¼ cup packed brown sugar

¼ teaspoon pure vanilla extract

6 tablespoons (¼ cup plus 2 tablespoons) self-rising flour

Pinch of kosher salt

1½ tablespoons caramel sauce store-bought or homemade (page 152)

METHOD

In a large mug, combine the pear and oil. Microwave for 30 seconds to warm through. Whisk in the egg with a fork. Stir in the milk, sugar, and vanilla. Add the flour and salt. Beat the batter until smooth. Swirl in the caramel sauce. Divide the batter between two mugs. Microwave separately for 1½ to 2½ minutes each until risen and firm.

Topping Ideas: Whipped cream, sour cream, caramel sauce, salted caramel sauce, pomegranate syrup, candied pecans, walnuts, freshly grated nutmeg, or cinnamon-sugar.

Variation: A great alternative to pears and caramel is pears and ginger. Omit the caramel sauce and replace it with a pinch of ground ginger, a tablespoon of peeled and grated fresh ginger, or ¼ cup of chopped candied ginger.

ginger-peach mug cake

There are several types of peaches—white, yellow, clingstone, freestone—and all are suitable for this recipe. Nectarines, the fuzz-free peaches, can be used here, too. Be sure to let it ripen all the way, so that its full peachy potential can shine.

INGREDIENTS

1 large egg

3½ tablespoons vegetable oil

3½ tablespoons buttermilk

¼ teaspoon pure vanilla extract

¼ cup packed brown sugar

6 tablespoons (¼ cup plus 2 tablespoons) self-rising flour

Pinch of kosher salt

½ teaspoon ground ginger

1 fresh peach, chopped, or ½ cup chopped canned peaches, drained

2 tablespoons chopped candied ginger or pecan pieces

METHOD

In a large mug, whisk together the egg and oil with a fork. Stir in the buttermilk, vanilla, and sugar. Add the flour, salt, and ginger. Beat the batter until smooth. Fold in the peaches and candied ginger. Divide the batter between two mugs. Microwave separately for 1½ to 2½ minutes each until risen and firm.

Topping Ideas: Whipped cream, crème fraîche, caramel sauce, candied pecans, or candied ginger.

plum-sage mug cake

MAKES 2 MUG CAKES

Spring and summer are the season for a wide variety of plums, the sweet-tart member of the stone fruit family that ranges in color from green and yellow to red and deep dark purple. The addition of sage gives this cake a piquant, savory tone that is mouthwateringly delicious.

INGREDIENTS

2 tablespoons unsalted butter

1 fresh plum, finely diced

2 teaspoons fresh sage leaves, minced (or ½ teaspoon ground sage)

1 large egg

3 tablespoons milk

¼ teaspoon pure vanilla extract

¼ cup granulated sugar

6 tablespoons (¼ cup plus 2 tablespoons) self-rising flour

Pinch of kosher salt

METHOD

In a large mug, combine the butter, plum, and sage. Microwave for 30 seconds until the butter is melted. Whisk in the egg with a fork. Stir in the milk, vanilla, and sugar. Add the flour and salt. Beat the batter until smooth. Divide the batter between two mugs. Microwave separately for 1½ to 2½ minutes each until risen and firm.

Variation: Sage is a lovely accompaniment to many fruits, including cherries, nectarines, and pineapple, as well as other classic pastry flavors like vanilla bean and caramel.

Topping Ideas: Whipped cream, crème fraîche, sour cream.

white chocolate–key lime mug cake

MAKES 2 MUG CAKES

Key limes, known as Mexican limes in some parts of the country, are not much bigger than a kumquat, and turn from green to yellow when ripe. If you can't find them, any lime will work here, as will bottled lime juice.

INGREDIENTS

1 large egg

1½ tablespoons vegetable oil

1 tablespoon sour cream

Finely grated zest of 2 key limes or 1 regular lime

2 tablespoons key lime juice

¼ cup granulated sugar

¼ cup self-rising flour

Pinch of kosher salt

¼ cup white chocolate chips

METHOD

In a large mug, whisk together the egg and oil with a fork. Stir in the sour cream, lime zest, lime juice, and sugar. Add the flour and salt. Beat the batter until smooth. Divide the batter between two mugs. Microwave separately for 30 seconds each. Top each mug with half of the chips, then continue to cook each mug for 1 to 1½ minutes more until risen and firm.

Topping Ideas: Lime glaze, lime curd, crème fraîche, shredded coconut, chopped macadamia nuts, candied lime zest, or a wedge of lime.

persimmon mug cake

MAKES 2 MUG CAKES

The persimmon is sometimes known as the lantern fruit because the leaves fall off the tree in the autumn and the ripe orange fruit is left hanging. There are two types of persimmon and both are suitable for baking. The heart-shaped Hachiya is an astringent persimmon, which remains extremely tannic until it is fully ripened and soft. The Fuyu is the tomato-shaped, nonastringent variety, which becomes sweet while still firm.

INGREDIENTS

2 tablespoons raisins and/or currants

1 tablespoon rum

2 tablespoons unsalted butter

¼ cup mashed or chopped persimmon pulp

1 large egg

3 tablespoons buttermilk

¼ teaspoon pure vanilla extract

¼ cup granulated sugar

6 tablespoons (¼ cup plus 2 tablespoons) self-rising flour

Pinch of freshly grated nutmeg

Pinch of kosher salt

2 tablespoons chopped pecans or walnuts

METHOD

In a large mug, combine the raisins, currants, and rum. Microwave for 30 seconds. Set aside for 10 to 30 minutes to allow the raisins and currants to plump.

In a second mug, combine the butter and persimmon. Microwave for 30 seconds until the butter is melted. Whisk in the egg with a fork. Stir in the buttermilk, vanilla, and sugar. Add the flour, nutmeg, and salt. Beat the batter until smooth. Fold in the raisins and/or currants and chopped nuts. Divide the batter between two mugs. Microwave separately for 1½ to 2½ minutes each until risen and firm.

Topping Ideas: Whipped cream, caramel cream, caramel sauce, rum hard sauce, rum-raisin glaze, freshly grated nutmeg, chopped pecans or walnuts.

nuts to you

there is no food that is better packaged, and has a more ancient and elegant history, than the nut. Within its shell lies concentrated nutrition that is rivaled only by the egg. Nuts have sustained human culture for millennia. Some of man's first tools were developed to crack open nuts during the Pleistocene era. Ancient Roman nut recipes abound in Apicius (a collection of ancient Roman recipes), native tribes of the Americas relied on them as staples, and the Victorians considered the cracking of dessert nuts an important social ritual.

Nuts are a staple in professional kitchens, and are an important ingredient to have on hand at home for baking and snacking. If you don't go through nuts quickly, store them in the freezer to prevent their high oil content from turning them rancid. See page 9 for instructions on how to toast nuts.

white chocolate–macadamia mug cake

MAKES 2 MUG CAKES

Although the pairing of a buttery, rich nut and buttery, rich chocolate seems counterintuitive, it actually works. Plop them into the batter after the cake has cooked a bit to prevent sinkage.

INGREDIENTS

1 large egg

3½ tablespoons vegetable oil

3½ tablespoons buttermilk

¼ cup granulated sugar

¼ teaspoon pure vanilla extract

5 tablespoons (¼ cup plus 1 tablespoon) self-rising flour

Pinch of kosher salt

¼ cup white chocolate chips

¼ cup chopped macadamia nuts

METHOD

In a large mug, whisk together the egg and oil with a fork. Stir in the buttermilk, sugar, and vanilla. Add the flour and salt. Beat the batter until smooth. Divide the batter between two mugs. Microwave separately for 30 seconds each. Top each mug with half of the chips and nuts, then continue to cook each mug for 1 to 1½ minutes more until risen and firm.

Topping Ideas: Whipped cream, crème fraîche, chopped macadamia nuts, shredded coconut, grilled pineapple sauce, fresh mango, fresh papaya, candied citrus zest, or a wedge of lime.

hazelnut-nutella mug cake

Nutella, which is made from ground hazelnuts, cocoa, and milk was first developed in Italy during World War II as a way to extend rationed chocolate. The combination of milk chocolate and hazelnuts can also be found in *gianduja*, a delicious alternative to milk chocolate, available for baking and in candy bars.

INGREDIENTS

2 tablespoons unsalted butter

¼ cup Nutella

1 large egg

2 tablespoons milk

1 teaspoon pure vanilla extract

3 tablespoons granulated sugar

6 tablespoons (¼ cup plus 2 tablespoons) self-rising flour

Pinch of kosher salt

¼ cup chopped hazelnuts preferably toasted (page 9) (optional)

METHOD

In a large mug, combine the butter and Nutella. Microwave for 20 to 30 seconds until melted. Whisk in the egg with a fork. Stir in the milk, vanilla, and sugar. Add the flour and salt. Beat the batter until smooth. Fold in the hazelnuts. Divide the batter between two mugs. Microwave separately for 1½ to 2½ minutes each until risen and firm.

Topping Ideas: Whipped cream, Nutella, Marshmallow Fluff, milk chocolate ganache, caramel sauce, confectioners' sugar, chopped hazelnuts, or fresh raspberries.

black walnut-black pepper mug cake

MAKES 2 MUG CAKES

With a more robust flavor than the common English walnut, black walnuts are preferred in commercial baking, pastry, and ice cream production. They are more common on the East Coast, where the tree originated. If you live outside of black walnut territory, use any walnut you can get your hands on. Black walnut extract is a grand alternative, and is available through a number of Internet sources. The pepper in this recipe complements the distinctive black walnut flavor, and adds a touch of heat. But feel free to leave it out if you're chicken ("bawk bawk!").

INGREDIENTS

2 tablespoons unsalted butter

½ cup black walnuts, finely chopped, preferably toasted (see page 8.)

1 large egg

3 tablespoons milk

1 teaspoon pure vanilla extract

¼ cup granulated sugar

6 tablespoons (¼ cup plus 2 tablespoons) self-rising flour

Pinch of kosher salt

¼ teaspoon freshly ground black pepper (4 to 5 twists of the pepper mill)

METHOD

Combine the butter and walnuts in a large mug. Microwave for 30 seconds until the butter is melted. Whisk with a fork to combine, then whisk in the egg. Stir in the milk, vanilla, and sugar. Add the flour, salt, and pepper. Beat the batter until smooth. Divide the batter between two mugs. Microwave separately for 1½ to 2½ minutes each until risen and firm.

Topping Ideas: Whipped cream, crème fraîche, maple frosting, hard sauce, caramel sauce, cinnamon-sugar, candied walnuts, sautéed apples, or sautéed bananas.

Variations

APPLE-WALNUT MUG CAKE: Add 1 grated apple to the butter mixture, then add a pinch of ground cinnamon to replace the pepper.

CARAMEL, WALNUT, AND PEPPER MUG CAKE: Fold in 2 tablespoons of caramel sauce, store-bought or homemade (page 152) before dividing the batter between the mugs.

PEPPER, PORT, FIG, AND WALNUT MUG CAKE: Add 2 chopped fresh figs to the butter mixture, and replace the milk with good-quality port wine.

WALNUT, PEPPER, AND DATE MUG CAKE: Add ¼ cup of chopped dates to the butter mixture.

coconut mug cake

MAKES 2 MUG CAKES

The coconut flourishes in the moist tropics, and it is the world's most useful plant. The coconut meat, water, oil, and hearts of palm are all edible, and the wood, roots, leaves, husks, and shells all have multiple, traditional uses. The best way to use coconut, however, is to fill your tummy.

INGREDIENTS

1 large egg

3 tablespoons canned unsweetened coconut milk

¼ teaspoon pure vanilla extract

¼ teaspoon coconut extract

¼ cup granulated sugar

⅓ cup self-rising flour

Pinch of kosher salt

¼ cup shredded coconut, preferably toasted (sweetened or unsweetened)

METHOD

In a large mug, whisk the egg with a fork. Stir in the coconut milk, extracts, and sugar. Add the flour and salt. Beat the batter until smooth. Fold in the shredded coconut. Divide the batter between two mugs. Microwave separately for 1½ to 2½ minutes each until risen and firm.

Topping Ideas: Whipped cream, coconut cream, Marshmallow Fluff, caramel sauce, chocolate sauce, rum glaze, lime glaze, grilled pineapple sauce, chopped macadamia nuts, shaved chocolate, or freshly grated nutmeg.

Note: If you don't have access to canned coconut milk, regular cow's milk will suffice, although it will reduce the coconutty-ness of this mug.

marzipan–almond mug cake

MAKES 2 MUG CAKES

Marzipan is a paste made from ground almonds and sugar. It is commonly colored and molded into fanciful shapes, but it is also used as a sweet, nutty ingredient, adding moisture and richness to a number of classic pastries. It is sold in 7-ounce tubes, and is available in most supermarket baking aisles. Almond paste, a similar product, can be used interchangeably here, with similar results. It is made for baking, not modeling, and is therefore a bit coarser.

INGREDIENTS

3 tablespoons marzipan or almond paste

Finely grated zest of 1 small lemon or orange

1 tablespoon unsalted butter

1 large egg

¼ cup milk

¼ teaspoon pure vanilla extract

3 tablespoons granulated sugar

⅓ cup self-rising flour

Pinch of kosher salt

2 to 4 tablespoons sliced almonds, preferably toasted (page 9)

METHOD

In a large mug, combine the marzipan, zest, and butter. Microwave for 20 seconds until softened. Whisk in the egg with a fork. Stir in the milk, vanilla, and sugar. Add the flour and salt. Beat the batter until smooth. Fold in the almonds. Divide the batter between two mugs. Microwave separately for 1½ to 2½ minutes each until risen and firm.

Topping Ideas: Whipped cream or crème fraîche, orange glaze, caramel sauce, sliced almonds, sliced apricots, or candied citrus zest.

sesame-cashew mug cake

MAKES 2 MUG CAKES

The cashew nut is actually a seed that grows off the end of the cashew apple, a sweet, delicate, tropical fruit commonly made into a fruity drink in the tree's native South America. Cashew nut paste is used frequently in Indian curries, and the whole nut appears in recipes throughout China and Southeast Asia. In the United States we see it mainly in nut mixes, and in bad sneezing jokes.

INGREDIENTS

1 large egg

2 tablespoons vegetable oil

½ teaspoon sesame oil

2 tablespoons milk

3 tablespoons granulated sugar

6 tablespoons (¼ cup plus 2 tablespoons) self-rising flour

Pinch of ground ginger

Pinch of kosher salt

1 tablespoon black or white sesame seeds, preferably toasted (page 9)

¼ cup chopped cashew nuts

METHOD

In a large mug, whisk together the egg and oils with a fork. Stir in the milk and sugar. Add the flour, ginger, salt, and sesame seeds. Beat the batter until it is smooth. Fold in the cashews. Divide the batter between two mugs. Microwave separately for 1½ to 2½ minutes each until risen and firm.

Topping Ideas: Whipped cream, green tea whipped cream, coconut whipped cream, sour cream, candied ginger, lychee nuts, kiwi fruit, or freshly grated nutmeg.

HOW TO TOAST SEEDS

The best way to toast seeds is in a small, dry sauté pan on the stovetop. Heat the pan, add the seeds, then toss them around continuously until their color darkens and you can smell them. Immediately pour them out of the hot pan and let them cool (it will only take a minute or two) before adding them to your recipe.

9
Celebrate!

Cakes are appropriate any day of the week, but the fact is, most people only bake for special occasions. This chapter is designed especially for the holidays, whichever holiday you decide to celebrate.

Baking for anything besides daily sustenance began for the worship of pagan or nature deities. Food presented on an altar as sacrifice or appeasement was a universal practice in all early civilizations. Today we continue to bake special cakes throughout the year, whether or not we are aware of their original meaning. Gingerbread, wedding cakes, King's cake, pannetone, stolen, kulich, challah, and fruitcakes all have spiritual origins, and are still enjoyed today in celebration of spiritual events.

Thanks to trains, airplanes, electricity, and the printing press we can bake whenever we want. And since we have much more to celebrate now than our Neolithic brethren did, every day is a great day for cake.

george washington mug cake

President's Day is the perfect excuse to make a mug cake. George Washington is often associated with cherries (although the tree-chopping thing is apocryphal), but in mid-twentieth-century Philadelphia there were several bakeries, including the beloved Haegele's and Hanscom's, selling something called a George Washington cake, which was essentially a chocolate-spice cake with chocolate icing. Some versions had apples, some even had a pastry crust, but all were delicious, and are fondly remembered by Philadelphians.

INGREDIENTS

2 tablespoons unsalted butter

½ teaspoon ground cinnamon

¼ teaspoon freshly grated nutmeg

1 unpeeled apple, grated (see Note page 24)

1 large egg

2 tablespoons milk

1 teaspoon pure vanilla extract

¼ cup granulated sugar

¼ cup self-rising flour

2 tablespoons unsweetened cocoa powder

Pinch of kosher salt

¼ cup toasted walnuts, chopped

METHOD

In a large mug, combine the butter, cinnamon, nutmeg, and grated apple. Microwave for 30 seconds until the butter is melted. Whisk in the egg with a fork. Stir in the milk, vanilla, and sugar. Add the flour, cocoa, and salt. Beat the batter until smooth. Fold in the walnuts. Divide the mixture between 2 mugs. Microwave separately for 1½ to 2½ minutes each until risen and firm.

Topping Ideas: Chocolate fudge icing, whipped cream, chopped walnuts, caramel sauce, confectioners' sugar, shaved chocolate, cinnamon-sugar, or freshly grated nutmeg.

shamrock mug cake

MAKES 2 MUG CAKES

Food coloring is not always a welcome ingredient, but this cake is a much beloved component of March 17th celebrations—especially if you're feeding little leprechauns. For the bigger leprechauns, omit the peppermint and add a tablespoon or three of Jameson's Irish whiskey.

INGREDIENTS

1 large egg

3 tablespoons vegetable oil

¼ cup granulated sugar

½ teaspoon pure vanilla extract

1 teaspoon liquid green food coloring

3 tablespoons buttermilk

1 drop peppermint extract (or 2 to 3 tablespoons Irish whiskey)

⅓ cup self-rising flour

Pinch of kosher salt

METHOD

In a large mug, whisk together the egg and oils with a fork. Stir in the sugar, vanilla, food coloring, buttermilk, and peppermint or whiskey. Add the flour and salt. Beat the batter until smooth. Divide the batter between two mugs. Microwave separately for 1½ to 2½ minutes each until risen and firm.

Topping Ideas: Cream cheese frosting (tinted green, perhaps?), green crystal sugar, Irish whiskey glaze, chiffonade of peppermint leaves, or shaved chocolate.

passover flourless chocolate mug cake

MAKES 1 MUG CAKE

Flourless chocolate cake is a time-honored Passover tradition, but you need not reserve it for the holiday. This mug cake is rich and decadent and will relieve your deep dark chocolate craving. If you keep kosher, use kosher chocolate, a parve butter substitute, or vegetable oil.

INGREDIENTS

3 tablespoons unsalted butter

¼ cup good-quality dark chocolate, cut into small pieces

1 large egg

1 teaspoon pure vanilla extract

3 tablespoons granulated sugar

2 tablespoons unsweetened cocoa powder

Pinch of kosher salt

METHOD

In a large mug, combine the butter and chocolate. Microwave for 30 to 60 seconds until melted. Whisk in the egg with a fork. Stir in the vanilla and sugar. Add the cocoa and salt. Beat the batter until smooth. Microwave the cake for 1½ to 2½ minutes until risen and firm.

Topping Ideas: A dusting of cocoa powder, confectioners' sugar, a few fresh berries, nondairy topping, crème fraîche, or whipped cream.

Note: If you prefer your flourless cake a little more cakey, stir in 2 tablespoons of matzo flour or almond flour.

red, white, and blueberry mug cake

MAKES 2 MUG CAKES

This dessert is a cliché because Independence Day happens to fall in the heart of berry season. Everyone expects it, so please "The People" and serve it up.

INGREDIENTS

2 tablespoons unsalted butter, softened

¼ cup granulated sugar

1 large egg

2 tablespoons milk

2 teaspoons pure vanilla extract

6 tablespoons (¼ cup plus 2 tablespoons) self-rising flour

Pinch of kosher salt

3 tablespoons strawberries or raspberries

3 tablespoons blueberries or blackberries

Variation: To play up the fruitiness of this mug cake, add the grated zest of 1 lemon or orange to the batter.

METHOD

In a large mug, whisk together the butter and sugar with a fork. Whisk in the egg. Stir in the milk and vanilla. Add the flour and salt. Beat the batter until smooth. Fold in the berries. Divide the batter between two mugs. Microwave separately for 1½ to 2½ minutes each until risen and firm.

caramel apple mug cake

MAKES 2 MUG CAKES

A tried-and-true Halloween party favorite, the caramel apple is perhaps one of the best ideas in history. Cloyingly sweet caramel tempered by a crisp, tart apple—whoever thought this up was a genius. Try it with pears, too, for a more sophisticated twist on this childhood favorite.

INGREDIENTS

2 tablespoons unsalted butter

1 unpeeled apple, grated (see Note page 24)

¼ teaspoon ground cinnamon

1 large egg

2 tablespoons milk

1 teaspoon pure vanilla extract

¼ cup granulated sugar

6 tablespoons (¼ cup plus 2 tablespoons) self-rising flour

Pinch of kosher salt

¼ cup caramel sauce store bought or homemade (page 152), or 4 chewy caramel candies

METHOD

In a large mug, combine the butter, apple, and cinnamon. Microwave for 30 seconds until the butter is melted. Whisk in the egg with a fork. Stir in the milk, vanilla, and sugar. Add the flour and salt. Beat the batter until smooth. Fold in the caramel sauce or candies. Divide the batter between 2 mugs. Microwave separately for 1½ to 2½ minutes each until risen and firm.

Topping Ideas: Whipped cream, crème fraîche, maple glaze, penuche frosting, candy corn, cinnamon-sugar, raisins, dried cranberries, or caramel sauce.

pumpkin spice mug cake

MAKES 2 MUG CAKES

Throw on your Snuggie and curl up with this autumnal favorite. The pumpkin puree can come from a can, or you can make it yourself by boiling diced pumpkin or butternut squash until tender, then mashing it with a fork. Of course, if you're into mug cakes, homemade pumpkin purée probably isn't in your bailiwick. In that case, for supereasy pumpkin puree, buy butternut squash baby food. (I won't tell anyone.)

INGREDIENTS

1 large egg

¼ cup pumpkin puree

2 tablespoons milk

¼ teaspoon pure vanilla extract

¼ cup packed brown sugar

7 tablespoons (¼ cup plus 3 tablespoons) self-rising flour

Pinch of kosher salt

½ teaspoon pumpkin pie spice (or ⅛ teaspoon each ground cinnamon, nutmeg, ginger, and a very tiny pinch of clove)

3 tablespoons toasted pecans or walnuts, chopped (optional) (page 9)

METHOD

In a large mug, whisk together the egg and pumpkin puree with a fork. Stir in the milk, vanilla, and sugar. Add the flour, salt, and spices. Beat the batter until smooth. Fold in the nuts. Divide the batter between two mugs. Microwave separately for 1½ to 2½ minutes each until risen and firm.

Topping Ideas: Whipped cream, maple whipped cream, Nutella whipped cream, penuche frosting, hard sauce, caramel sauce, freshly grated nutmeg, dried cranberries, or candied walnuts.

choco-peppermint mug cake

MAKES 2 MUG CAKES

Chocolate and mint are a great combination, and there is no better source of pepper-mint flavor than the candy cane. For this recipe, place a cane or two in a ziplock bag and crush with a hammer or meat mallet.

INGREDIENTS

2 tablespoons unsalted butter

¼ cup dark chocolate chips (semisweet or bittersweet)

1 large egg

3½ tablespoons milk

¼ cup granulated sugar

2 tablespoons self-rising flour

2 tablespoons unsweetened cocoa powder

Pinch of kosher salt

¼ cup crushed candy canes

Topping Ideas: Whipped cream, vanilla frosting, chocolate ganache, crushed peppermint sticks, shaved chocolate, or crumbled gingersnaps.

METHOD

Combine the butter and chocolate chips in a large mug. Microwave for 30 to 60 seconds until melted. Whisk with a fork to combine, then whisk in the egg. Stir in the milk and sugar. Add the flour, cocoa, and salt. Beat the batter until smooth. Fold in the crushed candy canes. Divide the batter between 2 mugs. Microwave separately for 1½ to 2½ minutes each until risen and firm.

for the sensitive ones

any cake in this book can be made to accommodate special diets. Substitutions are easy, and with the occasional adjustment, will produce mug cakes that are just as stupendous as the fully loaded versions. In addition to substitution instructions, you will also find a couple recipes in each category to get you started.

GLUTEN-FREE

Gluten-free cakes are created by swapping out wheat flour for a gluten-free flour, of which there are several. Most health food stores, and a growing number of mainstream markets, have gluten-free sections that stock a variety of alternative flours. No other flour acts the same as wheat flour, but with the variety available today, gluten-free baking comes pretty close to the original.

If you are new to gluten-free baking, try the packaged flour blends first. Once you get a sense for what is out there, you can start blending your own, using the variety of gluten-free flours available. These include amaranth flour, barley flour, brown rice flour, buckwheat flour, coconut flour, millet flour, oat flour, potato flour, quinoa flour, and a variety of legume and nut flours. They all have pronounced flavors that will impact your recipes, and for that reason blending them produces better cakes.

Unless you bake every day, keep specialty flours in the freezer. They have not been stripped of natural oils like processed white flours have, and are therefore subject to rancidity. (They will not freeze solid! They'll just be very cold.)

Because most of the recipes in this book use self-rising flour for convenience, you'll need to add baking powder to leaven gluten-free flour. Blend ¾ teaspoon of baking powder and a pinch of salt into a cup of gluten-free flour, then measure out your mug cake flour as needed. Make this mixture in bulk and store in the freezer so you'll be mug-ready at a moment's notice.

SUGAR-FREE

The one essential characteristic of a mug cake is that it is sweet. If it's not sweet, there's really no point. But sweet does not have to mean granulated, refined, processed white sugar. There are naturally sweet foods that are not processed, but are still considered "sugar" because they contain other forms of sugar, including dextrose, glucose, fructose, lactose, sorghum, galactose, invert sugar, or maltose. Sugar alternatives offer several health benefits, including a lower glycemic index, which means they enter your bloodstream more slowly, helping to minimize the sugar "crash." In addition, most alternatives contain vitamins, minerals, proteins, fats, and fiber, all of which are completely absent from refined white sugar.

Honey

Twice as sweet as sucrose, honey has a unique flavor that enhances baked goods and helps retain moisture. It is rich in antioxidants, and long-term use offers long-term health benefits, including improved digestion, a stronger immune system, and lower cholesterol. There are even some studies that indicate prolonged use of honey can minimize plant-based allergy symptoms.

When substituting honey in a recipe, start by using half of the amount given for sugar. Some honeys are less sweet, and might require as much as 75 percent of the initial recipe's sugar measurement, so it will take a little experimentation on your part.

Date Sugar

Date sugar is nothing but ground dried dates. It is equally as sweet as refined sugar, with the added benefit of fiber, which slows down its absorption into your body. As a bonus, date sugar also has all the vitamins and minerals of dates. It is terrific in cakes, and wherever you shake sugar for sweet crunchy toppings. However, because it does not melt like sugar, it's a bad choice for your morning coffee.

Maple Syrup

The majority of pancake syrups on the market are mostly corn syrup, but the real thing is made from reduced maple sap. Not only does it taste better, but it is also full of minerals and antioxidants. Grade A maple syrup is light in color. Grade B is darker, with a more concentrated flavor. Because it is a little less sweet than granulated sugar, replace the sugar measurement with an extra 25 percent of maple syrup. (Replace ¼ cup of sugar with ¼ cup plus 1 tablespoon of maple syrup.)

Unrefined Cane Sugar

This is sugar from sugar cane, extracted naturally, retaining all of its vitamins and minerals. It comes in both sugar and syrup forms. It is a little toastier and milder than maple syrup. Use either form as a replacement for granulated sugar in equal amounts.

Agave Nectar

From the same plant that brings us tequila comes this syrup, about as sweet as honey, but with a milder flavor and a lower glycemic index. When using it as a substitute for sugar, use two-thirds of the measurement given for granulated sugar. (Replace ¼ cup of granulated sugar with 2 tablespoons and 2 teaspoons of agave syrup.)

Stevia

This sweetener is extracted from an herb called sweetleaf or sugarleaf. It is three hundred times sweeter than granulated sugar, but has a glycemic index of zero. This means it will not affect your blood sugar level, and you won't get any sugar highs or lows. Because it is so highly concentrated, a pinch is all that is needed in a mug cake. Some folks report a slight anise or black licorice flavor.

Artificial Sweeteners

Also called non-nutritive sweeteners, there are five products that the Food and Drug Administration (FDA) has approved for human consumption. Testing is ongoing with all of these products, so health and safety are still in question. These products are easy to use, but be aware of side effects from excessive consumption.

Saccharine

Used as an artificial sweetener for over a hundred years, saccharine is over two hundred times sweeter than sucrose, and it doesn't raise blood sugar levels. But in the 1970s it was found to cause cancer in rats, and a ban was proposed. Because the effect has not been seen in humans, the product is still in use, but the labels of products containing saccharine must carry a warning. Sold as Sweet'N Low, six 1-gram packets will replace ¼ cup of granulated sugar.

Aspartame

Sold as Equal and NutraSweet, this artificial sweetener loses its sweetening power when it is heated, and for that reason is not recommended for baking. It's just as well, because there have been several claims of adverse health effects from aspartame, including headaches, dizziness, anxiety, cramps, multiple sclerosis, lupus, and cancer. Dieters have also reported that aspartame increases appetite.

Acesulfame Potassium K
Two hundred times sweeter than sucrose, this product is generally used as a flavor enhancer and preservative. Sold as Sweet One and Sunet, six 1-gram packets will replace ¼ cup of granulated sugar. It contains the carcinogen methylene chloride, which, with long exposure, causes headaches, nausea, depression, liver and kidney disease, and cancer in humans.

Sucralose
Sold as Splenda, this sweetener is six hundred times sweeter than sucrose, but is available in a granular formula that can be substituted for sugar cup for cup. Reports indicate it was discovered while treating sugar with a dozen chemicals to create an insecticide. It is not metabolized in the body like sugar, and adverse affects include gastrointestinal disorders, skin irritation, chest pain, anxiety, and depression.

Neotame
This is a new, sweeter version of aspartame, over 7,000 to 13,000 times sweeter than granulated sugar. The FDA has given initial approval, but it is not widely available to consumers, and studies continue.

DAIRY-FREE
There are lots of great dairy alternatives for vegans and the lactose intolerant, including soy milk, rice milk, almond milk, coconut milk, oat milk, and even potato milk. They are all available in several flavors, and can all be used cup for cup to replace the dairy in a recipe.

To replace sour cream or buttermilk, try a soy-based sour cream substitute for the closest texture and flavor. Replace cup for cup.

Coconut oil is a great trans fat-free butter replacement. Solid at room temperature, coconut oil is a natural product with a slight coconut flavor. Margarine can be dairy-free, but check the ingredient label for sodium caseinate, which is a milk derivative.

VEGAN

The biggest obstacle for vegan baking is the egg. The protein of an egg solidifies to hold a baked product together, the fat in the egg retains moisture and, in certain preparations, the egg assists in leavening either through the accumulation of air or the release of steam. Without it, cakes are dense, flat, and dry. Luckily, there are several options for egg substitution, both homemade and store-bought.

Easiest, by far, are the store-bought egg replacers. Powdered egg replacers are generally made of a combination of starches, leaveners, and gums. They work great, especially for baking. Follow the ratio on the box as they vary slightly (although generally 1 tablespoon replacer + ¼ cup water = 1 egg.)

There are also a few homemade versions, including the popular flaxseed replacement. Grind flaxseeds in a coffee mill, then blend them with water. (1 tablespoon milled flaxseed pureed with 3 tablespoons water = 1 egg.) The mixture thickens within a few minutes, and can be stored in the fridge for several days.

Starch is a common egg replacer, although the results are not as good for baking. (2 tablespoons of cornstarch, potato starch, or arrowroot, dissolved in 2 tablespoons cold water = 1 egg.)

Gluten-Free **gf**   Sugar-Free **sf**   Dairy-Free **df**   Vegan **v**

chocolate mug cake

MAKES 2 MUG CAKES

Gluten-free diets have become somewhat of a trend. There are, however, people that become ill when they eat gluten. This mug cake recipe is for those folks. Once you decide that you love this cake, start experimenting with the rest of this book's recipes. You've been deprived of cake for too long.

INGREDIENTS

¼ cup unsalted butter

⅓ cup dark chocolate chips (semisweet or bittersweet)

1 large egg

2 tablespoons granulated sugar

1 teaspoon pure vanilla extract

2 tablespoons amaranth flour

1 tablespoon brown rice flour

⅛ teaspoon baking powder

Pinch of kosher salt

METHOD

In a large mug combine the butter and chocolate chips. Microwave for 30 seconds until melted. Stir with a fork to combine, then whisk in the egg. Stir in the sugar and vanilla. Add the flour, baking powder, and salt. Beat the batter until smooth. Fold in the almonds. Divide the batter between two mugs. Microwave separately for 1½ to 2 minutes each until risen and firm.

Topping Ideas: Whipped cream, chocolate whipped cream, chocolate ganache, chocolate sauce, caramel sauce, fresh berries, or sliced stone fruits.

cocoa-banana mug cake

MAKES 2 MUG CAKES

This cake is gluten-free the way the North Pole is bikini-free. It's simply not needed. It's not as cakey as other recipes in this book, but it is certainly just as tasty.

INGREDIENTS

1 overripe banana

¼ cup peanut butter (or any nut butter)

1 large egg

2 teaspoons granulated sugar, or alternative sweetener (see sugar-free pages 98–101)

3 tablespoons unsweetened cocoa powder

¼ cup add-ins of your choice, including chocolate chips, chopped nuts, or dried fruits

METHOD

Mash the banana in a large mug with a fork. Add the nut butter and egg and mix thoroughly. Stir in the sugar and cocoa and beat until smooth. Fold in the add-ins. Divide the batter between two mugs. Microwave separately for 1½ to 2½ minutes each until risen and firm.

Topping Ideas:

Whipped cream, peanut butter–whipped cream, chocolate whipped cream, ganache, chocolate sauce, or candied nuts.

sesame-ginger mug cake

MAKES 2 MUG CAKES

Honey, sesame, and ginger combine for a classic Asian flavor trio. Enhance this combo by folding in fresh plums, apricots, or pineapple.

INGREDIENTS

1 large egg

2 tablespoons vegetable oil

3 tablespoons honey

2 tablespoons milk

6 tablespoons (¼ cup plus 2 tablespoons) self-rising flour

1 tablespoon peeled and grated fresh ginger (or 1 teaspoon ground ginger)

1 tablespoon toasted sesame seeds

Pinch of kosher salt

METHOD

In a large mug, whisk together the egg, oil, and honey with a fork. Stir in the milk. Add the flour, ginger, sesame seeds, and salt. Beat the batter until smooth. Divide the batter between two mugs. Microwave separately for 1½ to 2½ minutes each until risen and firm.

Topping Ideas: Whipped coconut cream (sweetened with honey), chopped almonds, or chopped cashews.

agave-lime mug cake

MAKES 2 MUG CAKES

Because it is made from the same plant that brings us tequila, it is no surprise that the flavors that complement tequila also complement agave syrup. But don't let that limit you. Agave is terrific wherever you need a little sweetness.

INGREDIENTS

2 tablespoons unsalted butter

Finely grated zest and juice of 1 lime

1 large egg

¼ cup agave syrup

2 tablespoons unsweetened coconut milk or sour cream

6 tablespoons (¼ cup plus 2 tablespoons) self-rising flour

Pinch of kosher salt

METHOD

In a large mug, combine the butter and lime zest. Microwave for 20 to 30 seconds until the butter is melted. Whisk in the egg with a fork. Stir in the lime juice, agave, and coconut milk. Add the flour and salt. Beat the batter until smooth. Divide the batter between two mugs. Microwave separately for 1½ to 2½ minutes each until risen and firm.

Topping Ideas: Agave-sweetened whipped cream, coconut whipped cream, sliced bananas, or sliced mango.

almond-lavender mug cake

MAKES 2 MUG CAKES

Lavender is a common ingredient throughout the Mediterranean, and a crucial element in the herb blend *herbes de Provence*. It can be bought in bulk at Indian, Middle Eastern, and sometimes Mexican markets. It can also be picked from a garden near you! Once you have the buds, crush them to release their fragrant oils.

INGREDIENTS

1 large egg

2 tablespoons vegetable oil

1 tablespoon edible lavender flowers, crushed, or pulverized in a coffee mill or mortar

3 tablespoons almond milk

¼ cup granulated sugar

6 tablespoons (¼ cup plus 2 tablespoons) self-rising flour

Pinch of kosher salt

¼ cup chopped almonds

METHOD

In a large mug, whisk together the egg, oil, and lavender with a fork. Stir in the almond milk and sugar. Add the flour and salt. Beat the batter until smooth. Fold in the almonds. Divide the batter between two mugs. Microwave separately for 1½ to 2½ minutes each until risen and firm.

Topping Ideas: Nondairy whipped topping, confectioners' sugar, candied edible flower petals, or chopped almonds.

sour cream, apple, and pecan mug cake

MAKES 2 MUG CAKES

Sour cream has a tang similar to buttermilk, which is a lovely match to apples and toasted pecans. Use a soy-based sour cream substitute to make this recipe dairy-free. See Dairy-Free, page 101.

INGREDIENTS

1 small apple, grated (see Note page 24)

2 tablespoons vegetable oil

1 large egg

3 tablespoons soy-based sour cream (Tofutti makes a good one)

1 teaspoon vanilla extract

¼ cup granulated sugar

6 tablespoons (¼ cup plus 2 tablespoons) self-rising flour

1 teaspoon freshly grated nutmeg

Pinch of kosher salt

¼ cup chopped pecans, preferably toasted (page 9)

METHOD

In a large mug, combine the grated apple and oil. Microwave for 30 seconds to warm through. Whisk in the egg with a fork. Stir in the sour cream, vanilla, and sugar. Add the flour, nutmeg, and salt. Beat the batter until smooth. Fold in the pecans. Divide the batter between two mugs. Microwave separately for 1½ to 2½ minutes each until risen and firm.

Topping Ideas: Caramel sauce (see page 152), confectioners' sugar, sautéed apples, nondairy whipped topping.

sweet potato mug cake

Sweet potatoes are a superfood, full of vitamins, fiber, and flavor. Cook them just like a baked potato in the oven or microwave, boil them, or be super-sneaky and buy a jar of sweet potato baby food. No one will know but you, and you know it's wholesome!

INGREDIENTS

1 tablespoon egg substitute

¼ cup water

¼ cup mashed cooked sweet potatoes

2 tablespoons soy, rice, or almond milk

¼ teaspoon pure vanilla extract

¼ cup packed brown sugar

7 tablespoons (¼ cup plus 3 tablespoons) self-rising flour

Pinch of kosher salt

½ teaspoon ground cinnamon

½ teaspoon freshly grated nutmeg

½ teaspoon ground ginger

3 tablespoons toasted pecans or walnuts, chopped (optional)

METHOD

In a large mug, whisk together the egg substitute and water with a fork and set aside for 5 minutes to thicken. Stir in the sweet potato, soy milk, vanilla, and sugar. Add the flour, salt, and spices. Beat the batter until smooth. Fold in the nuts. Divide the batter between two mugs. Microwave separately for 1½ to 2½ minutes each until risen and firm.

Topping Ideas: Caramel sauce (see page 152), pomegranate syrup, nondairy whipped topping, toasted pumpkin seeds, or confectioners' sugar.

orange-chocolate mug cake

MAKES 1 MUG CAKE

This cake is so moist and delicious you can even serve it to your carnivorous friends.

INGREDIENTS

2 tablespoons vegetable oil

Finely grated zest of 1 orange

2 tablespoons fresh orange juice

¼ cup granulated sugar

2 tablespoons unsweetened cocoa powder

¼ cup self-rising flour

Pinch of kosher salt

METHOD

In a large mug, whisk together the oil, orange zest, orange juice, and sugar with a fork. Add the cocoa, flour, and salt. Beat the batter until smooth. Microwave the cake for 1½ to 2½ minutes until risen and firm.

Topping Ideas: Vegan cream cheese icing, caramel glaze, nondairy whipped topping, candied orange peel, or chopped almonds.

11

not exactly cakes

i t's hard to believe, but there may come a day when you are not in the mood for cake. It is at those times that you will find comfort in the knowledge that almost anything can be cooked in the mighty microwave. When it comes to small mug batches, anything is possible.

MUG CHEESECAKES

The trick to the microwave cheesecake is patience. It cooks fast, but is best when allowed to chill. If you are in a hurry (of course you are) put the finished mug in the freezer for 15 minutes. Otherwise, try making these before dinner and give them a chance to set up in the refrigerator for an hour.

MUG PUDDINGS

Pudding is the essence of comfort food, and is at its comfortable best when made with leftovers— the unwanted end of a loaf of bread, the extra container of rice from take-out Chinese, a few pieces of overripe fruit. Get creative, then get your slippers on and find the remote.

MUG PIES

Because pie dough is essentially flour held together by butter (which melts easily in the microwave) it is hard to imagine making pie in the microwave. There is a trick that will let you enjoy the Great American Pie Experience in a few minutes. Bake the dough directly from the freezer, frozen as solid as possible. In this way, the fat stays solid as the proteins solidify. As with all other microwave baking techniques, pie dough lacks the ability to brown, which is a good argument for using whole wheat flour, or topping your creations with confectioners' sugar, whipped cream, or ice cream á la mode.

MUG BARS

An essential component of the home-baker's *oeuvre*, bars are the mainstay of every bake sale and pot luck. They are quick and easy as bars, so imagine how crazy-great they are as mugs!

lindy's-style mug cheesecake

MAKES 2 MUG CHEESECAKES

Opened in 1921, the now-defunct Lindy's Deli on Broadway in New York City served the most famous cheesecake in America. Lindy's waiters were trained in the fine art of the snappy comeback, and their insults were as much of a draw as the cheesecake, bringing the likes of Groucho Marx and Milton Berle to their booths as regular customers. "Waiter, do you serve shrimps here?" "Sure, we don't care how tall you are."

INGREDIENTS

½ cup graham crackers, crumbled or crushed into small bits

1 tablespoon unsalted butter

8 ounces cream cheese

⅓ cup granulated sugar

Pinch of kosher salt

Finely grated zest and juice of 1 lemon

1 large egg

Topping Ideas: Sour cream glaze, whipped cream, crème fraîche, or fresh fruit.

METHOD

Divide the graham crackers between two large mugs. Top each with half of the butter. Microwave each mug separately for 20 seconds until the butter is melted. Stir the crumbs with a fork so they are well coated with butter. Set the mugs aside.

In a large bowl, beat together the cream cheese, sugar, and salt with a fork or large spoon until smooth and creamy. Add the lemon zest, lemon juice, and egg. Beat the batter until smooth. Divide the batter between the two mugs. (Plop the mixture on top of the graham crackers, and give each mug a little tap to settle the cheese mixture.) Microwave separately for 1½ to 2½ minutes each until the filling is slightly puffed.

Remove each mug from the microwave and chill for 15 to 60 minutes for full enjoyment.

Variations

PUMPKIN-GINGERSNAP CHEESECAKE: Replace the graham crackers with crumbled gingersnap cookies. Omit the lemon and replace it with ¼ cup of pumpkin puree and a pinch of pumpkin pie spice (cinnamon, ginger, nutmeg, and cloves).

OREO CHEESECAKE: Replace the graham crackers with crumbled Oreo cookies. Omit the butter, because the creamy filling has enough fat to bind the crumbs. Fold the crumbled cookies into the cheesecake batter, too, if you dare.

mug bread pudding

MAKES 2 MUG PUDDINGS

Bread is the X-factor in bread pudding. Any bread will work, but the general rule is that the richer the bread, the richer (or better) the bread pudding. A stale French baguette works, as does your regular sandwich bread, stale croissants, yesterday's Danish, or that last donut everyone wanted but was afraid to take. Waste not, want not.

INGREDIENTS

1 large egg

¼ cup granulated sugar

1 cup milk

½ teaspoon pure vanilla extract

Pinch of kosher salt

Pinch of ground cinnamon

1½ cups stale bread cubes

Topping Ideas: Whipped cream, cinnamon-sugar, or fresh fruit.

METHOD

In a medium bowl, whisk together the egg and sugar with a fork. Stir in the milk, vanilla, salt, and cinnamon. Add the bread cubes and toss so they are coated evenly with custard. If time allows, set aside the mixture to soak for 10 to 20 minutes. Divide the mixture between two large mugs. Pack the mixture in so that there is very little air between the bread cubes. Microwave separately for 1½ to 2½ minutes each until the custard is absorbed and the pudding is firm.

Variations

EXTRA-RICH BREAD PUDDING: If you want to live it up, replace the milk with heavy cream.

CARAMELIZED APPLE BREAD PUDDING: Add ½ cup of sautéed apples to the bread and custard mixture.

RUM-RAISIN BREAD PUDDING: Combine ½ cup of raisins with 2 tablespoons of rum and 2 tablespoons of water. Microwave for 30 seconds to warm through. Set aside at room temperature for 10 to 20 minutes to allow the raisins to plump, then add them to the bread and custard mixture.

BERRY BREAD PUDDING: Add ½ cup of fresh or frozen raspberries, blackberries, or blueberries to the bread and custard mixture.

GINGERBREAD EGGNOG PUDDING: Use leftover gingerbread (cookies or cake) as the base of this pudding, and replace the milk and egg with 1¼ cups of prepared eggnog.

SAVORY PUDDING: Omit the sugar, and add cheese. But switch up the bread, too. Try it with rye or pumpernickel, multigrain or olive bread. Then, add any savory garnish you can imagine, like roasted peppers, sautéed mushrooms, onions, or pesto.

mug rice pudding

There are two types of rice pudding—thick or soupy. This recipe is thick, but can be altered by adding a little more milk to please the soupy-pudding lovers. Like bread pudding, rice pudding is a way to use up leftovers. Any cooked rice will work, and the stickier the rice, the thicker the pudding will be. Or try this with alternative grains, like quinoa, spelt, or kamut—versions of sweet grain puddings are found across the globe, flavored in hundreds of ways. Use your imagination, and create the rice pudding of your dreams.

INGREDIENTS

1 large egg

¼ cup granulated sugar

1 cup milk

½ teaspoon pure vanilla extract

Pinch of kosher salt

Pinch of ground cinnamon

¼ cup raisins

2 cups cooked rice

Topping Ideas:
Whipped cream, confectioners' sugar, cinnamon-sugar, or fresh fruit.

METHOD

In a medium bowl, whisk together the egg and sugar with a fork. Stir in the milk, vanilla, salt, and cinnamon. Add the raisins and rice and stir them well so they are completely coated with custard. Divide the mixture between two large mugs. Microwave separately for 1½ to 2½ minutes each until the custard is absorbed and the pudding is firm. Serve warm or chilled.

Variations

EXTRA-RICH RICE PUDDING: For a more decadent version, replace the milk with heavy cream.

COCONUT-MANGO RICE PUDDING: Replace the milk with canned coconut milk, and replace the raisins with chopped mango.

MOCHA RICE PUDDING: Omit the raisins. Fold in 1 tablespoon of espresso powder and ½ cup of chocolate chips.

GINGER-ROSE RICE PUDDING: Omit the raisins. Replace the sugar with 3 tablespoons of honey. Add 1 tablespoon of rose water and ½ teaspoon of ground ginger or 1 teaspoon peeled and grated fresh ginger.

basic pie dough

Any pie dough will work using this frozen method, including the store-bought variety. But in case you cut class the day they taught this in Home Ec (or you were born after the demise of Home Ec), here is a great pie dough recipe that is suitable not only for mug pies, but traditional oven-baked pies as well. It makes more than you need for one mug, but it freezes well. If you make several mug-size disks they will be ready for your weekly late-night pie craving. (You have those too, right?)

INGREDIENTS

¼ cup ice water

1 teaspoon fresh lemon juice

1½ cups all-purpose or whole wheat flour

Pinch of kosher salt

1 tablespoon granulated sugar

8 tablespoons (1 stick) unsalted butter, diced and chilled

METHOD

Combine the water and lemon juice in a small cup and set aside. In a medium bowl, stir together the flour, salt, and sugar with a fork. Add the chilled, diced butter and break it into tiny pieces using a fork or your fingertips. The mixture should not be creamy, but dry and crumbly. Add half the water, and stir with the fork to moisten. Add enough additional water to just hold the dough together. The dough should appear somewhat marbled, with bits of flour and butter still visible. Press it into a disk, wrap in plastic wrap, and refrigerate for 1 hour. (The dough can be refrigerated for 2 days, or frozen for up to 1 month.)

To roll out the dough, divide it into 2 or 3 smaller pieces. Work with only one piece of the dough at a time and keep the remaining dough refrigerated. Knead the dough briefly to soften and flatten it into a disk. Place it on a floured surface and, using a rolling pin, roll over the center of the dough in one direction. Turn the dough 90 degrees and roll in the center again. Turn the dough again, and repeat this pattern until the dough is a ¼ inch thick. Turning the dough in this manner alerts you right away if it starts sticking to the counter. Spread flour under the dough as necessary to prevent sticking. Work quickly to prevent the dough from warming up.

Using a cookie or biscuit cutter, cut the dough into 3-inch circles. Using a fork, poke tiny decorative holes in each disk. This keeps them from bubbling up during baking. Place them in a single layer on a wax paper–lined baking sheet, wrap in plastic wrap, and freeze solid. As needed, bake as directed, using 1 disk of rolled out pie dough on the top of each mug pie.

apple–cheddar mug pie

MAKES 1 MUG PIE

Marie Callender's may not have a Michelin star, but they certainly know their pie. Their napkins read: "An apple pie without the cheese is like a kiss without a squeeze." They got that right. Any apple will work here, so choose one that you like to eat out of hand.

INGREDIENTS

1½ cups of peeled, cored, and thinly sliced apples

1 teaspoon unsalted butter

1 teaspoon brown sugar

Pinch of ground cinnamon

Pinch of kosher salt

½ teaspoon cornstarch

1 ounce sharp cheddar cheese

One 3-inch disk frozen pie dough

½ teaspoon cinnamon sugar

Topping Ideas: Just the cheese, please.

METHOD

In a large mug, combine the apple slices and butter. Microwave for 30 to 60 seconds until the fruit is tender. Stir in the sugar, cinnamon, salt, and cornstarch with a fork. Top the fruit with the cheddar cheese. On top of the cheese place a frozen disk of pie dough, and sprinkle it with cinnamon-sugar. Microwave the pie for 30 to 45 seconds more until the dough has set.

Note: A half-century ago apple varieties had very distinct differences. When cooked, the red ones turned to mush (perfect for applesauce), and the green ones stayed firm. But today apples are bred mainly for the lunch box, and most commercial varieties will remain whole throughout the cooking process.

boysenberry mug pie

MAKES 1 MUG PIE

The boysenberry, a cross between the raspberry, blackberry, and loganberry, was created by Rudolph Boysen. But it was nurtured to perfection by Walter Knott, who sold them at his now world-famous Berry Farm in Buena Park, California.

INGREDIENTS

1½ cups fresh boysenberries

1 teaspoon unsalted butter

2 teaspoons granulated sugar

Finely grated zest of ½ lemon

Pinch of kosher salt

½ teaspoon cornstarch

One 3-inch disk frozen pie dough

Topping Ideas: Vanilla ice cream, whipped cream, or confectioners' sugar.

METHOD

In a large mug, combine the berries and butter. Microwave for 30 seconds until the butter is melted and the fruit is warmed through. Stir in the sugar, zest, salt, and cornstarch with a fork. Top the fruit with a frozen disk of pie dough. Microwave the pie for 30 to 45 seconds until the dough has set.

Variation: There are many fruits that shine when baked into a mug cake. The best choices are berries (except strawberries, which are watery and turn pale), stone fruits (plums, nectarines, apricots, cherries), and mango. Watery fruits like melon or kiwi are a bad choice, and like strawberries, lose their color. Tart fruits like rhubarb, pineapple, cranberries, or red currants will work, but will need a big adjustment in sugar, which you will need to determine by taste.

pumpkin mug pie

This is a tried-and-true holiday favorite, but there is no law that says you need to reserve it for November. But if your pumpkin craving hits in April, and you have trouble finding pumpkin puree at the store, have no fear. Boil, roast, or microwave diced butternut squash or sweet potato, then mash it up with a fork. The effect is equally delicious.

INGREDIENTS

1 tablespoon unsalted butter

1 large egg

1 cup unsweetened 100 percent pure pumpkin puree

1 tablespoon brown sugar

½ teaspoon pumpkin pie spice (cinnamon, ginger, nutmeg, and cloves)

Pinch of kosher salt

½ teaspoon pure vanilla extract

1 tablespoon heavy cream

One 3-inch disk frozen pie dough

½ teaspoon cinnamon-sugar

Topping Ideas: Whipped cream is classic. Why mess with perfection?

METHOD

In a large mug, melt the butter in the microwave for 20 seconds. Whisk in the egg and the pumpkin puree with a fork. Stir in the sugar, spices, salt, vanilla, and cream. Beat the custard until smooth. Microwave for 30 to 60 seconds until the custard is set. Top the custard with a frozen disk of pie dough, and sprinkle it with cinnamon-sugar. Microwave the pie for 1 to 1½ minutes more until the dough has set.

Variation: If you prefer your pumpkin pie with a graham cracker crust, crumble a graham cracker into the bottom of each of two mugs. Add a teaspoon of butter and microwave each mug for 20 seconds until the butter is melted. Stir with a fork to coat the cracker crumbs with butter, plop the pumpkin custard (from the recipe above) on top, and microwave for 1 to 1½ minutes until the custard is set. Sure, pumpkin pie is a custard, and like other custards, it is best served chilled. Of course, if you are in a hurry, the freezer will cool things off in a jiffy.

peach crumb mug pie

MAKES 1 MUG PIE

Also known as a crisp, or crumble, the crumb pie uses streusel to simulate a top crust. It's so easy and good, it may permanently replace pie as you know it. Peaches star in this version, because there is nothing better than a fresh, ripe peach. (Nothing. Except maybe diamonds.) Unfortunately, such perfection is hard to come by most of the year. If peaches are out of season, frozen fruit is the next best thing. Most growers flash-freeze their peaches at the peak of ripeness right in the orchard. Canned peaches are much less desirable, as they are usually packed in sugary syrup, which is added hot, giving the peach a mushy, slimy texture. If you can't find fresh or frozen, your last resort is to opt for a different fruit.

INGREDIENTS

Streusel

½ cup all-purpose or whole wheat flour

2 tablespoons brown or granulated white sugar

2 tablespoons unsalted butter, cubed and chilled

Filling

1½ cups sliced ripe peaches

1 teaspoon unsalted butter

1 tablespoon brown sugar

Pinch of ground ginger

Pinch of kosher salt

½ teaspoon cornstarch

METHOD

In a large mug, whisk together the flour and sugar with a fork. Add the chilled butter and break it into small pieces using the fork or your fingertips until the mixture resembles a coarse meal. It should not be creamy, but dry and crumbly. Set the mixture aside in the fridge.

In a second mug, combine the peaches and butter. Microwave for 30 seconds until the butter is melted and the fruit is warmed through. Stir in the sugar, ginger, salt, and cornstarch with a fork. Top the fruit with a generous helping of streusel. Microwave for 1 to 1½ minutes until the fruit is bubbly and the streusel is set.

Variation: As with pastry-topped pies, this method works with any fruit that is not too watery. Blueberries, raspberries, blackberries, cherries, and rhubarb are all great choices. Firm fruits, like apples or pears, work best when sliced thinly and precooked until tender.

seven layer mug bar

MAKES 1 MUG BAR

If this doesn't curb your sweet tooth, nothing will.

INGREDIENTS

1 graham cracker, crushed
or crumbled

1 tablespoon unsalted
butter, softened

2 tablespoons sweetened
or unsweetened
shredded coconut

2 tablespoons dark
chocolate chips (semisweet
or bittersweet)

2 tablespoons
butterscotch chips

2 tablespoons white
chocolate chips

2 tablespoons pecan
pieces

¼ cup sweetened
condensed milk

METHOD

In a large mug (or two smaller mugs), layer the graham crackers, butter, coconut, chips, and nuts. Pour the condensed milk on top. Microwave the mug for 1 to 1½ minutes until the chocolates have melted. Allow the mug to cool to room temperature, or chill in the fridge for 10 minutes, before enjoying.

blondie mug bar

MAKES 2 MUG BARS

Blondies are nothing but chocolate chip cookies baked in a pan rather than scooped out individually. They are the lazy baker's homemade cookies. (But if that's true, what does that make the mug cake version?)

INGREDIENTS

3 tablespoons unsalted butter, softened

2 tablespoons granulated sugar

2 tablespoons brown sugar

Pinch of kosher salt

1 large egg

½ teaspoon pure vanilla extract

½ cup self-rising flour

¼ cup dark chocolate chips (semisweet or bittersweet)

METHOD

In a large mug, combine the butter and sugars. Mix thoroughly with a fork. Stir in the salt, egg, and vanilla. Add the flour, a little at a time, and beat the batter until smooth. Fold in chocolate chips. Divide the batter between two mugs. Microwave separately for 1 to 1½ minutes each until risen and firm.

Toppings Ideas: Vanilla ice cream or whipped cream.

Variation: Anything you add to your chocolate chip cookies can be added here, including spices, nuts, raisins, or different chocolate varieties.

lemon bar mug

Lemon bars are one of the best-selling bake sale items of all time, neck and neck with brownies for top honors. Like all the puddings, these benefit from a little chill.

INGREDIENTS

3 tablespoons unsalted butter

2 tablespoons graham cracker or vanilla wafer crumbs

1 large egg

¼ cup granulated sugar

Finely grated zest of 1 lemon

¼ cup fresh lemon juice

METHOD

In a large mug, cook the butter in the microwave for 30 seconds until melted. Transfer 2 tablespoons of the melted butter into a small bowl and set aside. Add cracker crumbs to the mug, and stir them with a fork to coat the crumbs with the remaining butter.

To the butter in the bowl, add the egg and whisk with a fork. Stir in the sugar, lemon zest, and lemon juice and mix thoroughly. Pour the lemon mixture into the mug on top of the cracker crumbs. (The crumbs will float . . . do not be alarmed.) Microwave the custard for 1 to 1½ minutes until set. Refrigerate for 10 to 15 minutes for maximum enjoyment. When cool, top the mug with a dusting of confectioners' sugar.

Variations

KEY LIME MUG BAR: Replace the lemon juice and zest with key lime juice and zest.

ORANGE MUG BAR: Replace 3 tablespoons of the lemon juice with orange or blood orange juice.

POMEGRANATE MUG BAR: Replace 3 tablespoons of the lemon juice with pomegranate juice. Sprinkle the top with pomegranate seeds before serving.

mug cake mixes for giving

Mug cake mixes make great homemade gifts. Any mug cake recipe in this book can be made into a mix by simply omitting the wet ingredients. Combine the self-rising flour, sugar, and spices, and any other dry ingredient that might be in the recipe (cocoa powder, citrus zest, chocolate chips, nuts, etc). Mix them together, then package them into decorative plastic bags that fit nicely into a large gift mug. Then create a recipe gift tag to tie on the top that includes the wet ingredients and the method. (Espresso Mug Cake recipe on page 46.)

ESPRESSO MUG CAKE INSTRUCTIONS

In a large mug, use a fork to combine the contents of this package with:

1 large egg
3 tablespoons vegetable oil
3 tablespoons milk

Divide the batter between 2 mugs and microwave each for 1½ to 2½ minutes, until they are risen and firm.

Top with whipped cream and cinnamon sugar

A few suggestions:

- Put the mix in a regular ziplock bag first. Remove all the air before closing, then place that bag into a taller decorative plastic gift bag. This way you can simply tie the gift bag with a ribbon without worrying that the powdered mix might leak out.
- Be sure to buy a mug that will hold your bag of mix. Tea cups are cute, but are usually too small for one mug cake recipe.
- Make a few bags of mug cake mix and store them in the freezer. They will keep nicely, and can be thrown into a decorative bag and gift mug in a hurry. Now you're ready for that last-minute hostess gift, or the secretary appreciation day you forgot about (again).

12

toppings
and
garnishes

the mug cake is, by definition, an on-the-fly kind of food. But that doesn't mean it has to be boring. If you are so inclined, there are a number of toppings that can drastically increase the wow-factor of your microwave magic.

Most (but not all) of these toppings can be mixed up in a mug, and instructions are given here in that manner. The recipes will make enough to generously top two mug cakes. If you find yourself wanting to make a standard-size cake, they can all be easily increased and made in the traditional manner, using a bowl, a mixer, a whisk, a stove, or an oven.

FROSTINGS

Confectioners' sugar holds a lot of liquid. A LOT. And different brands are more absorbent than others. Similarly, different brands of dairy products contain different amounts of water. And to make things even more confusing, the weather can affect the absorption rate. (Humidity, for example, will result in a need for added dry ingredients.) For that reason, the measurements for frosting recipes such as these are never 100 percent accurate. To combat this phenomenon, each method here ends by encouraging you to add a little more or less confectioners' sugar or liquid to get the consistency you need. In other words, don't be afraid to eyeball it.

CREAMS

Texture is an important element in dessert composition. The more textural difference a dish has, the more interesting it is to eat. When composing desserts for restaurant menus I will always include elements of varying textures—cakey, creamy, crispy, juicy, icy—as well as varied temperatures. Creaminess is the perfect accompaniment to cake. Just because it's coming out of a microwave doesn't mean you can't jazz it up. Even a humble mug cake can benefit from a textural counterpoint.

GLAZES

These toppings are thin, translucent, and just sweet enough to add a little sweet zip to your mug cake. Drizzle them over any cake you think deserves a little shine.

SAUCES

Sauces drizzled over a mug cake take your microwave creation from "I just whipped this up" to "I made this especially for you." Which one would you rather have?

Fruit Sauces

Any firm fruit can be made into a sauce by pureeing it in a blender. Food processors work, too, but are better used for large batches. (Small amounts of puree tend to spin at the edge of the bowl and avoid the blade.) Avoid fruits that are full of water, like melons. Sugar can be added, but the amount necessary depends on the fruit and how ripe it is. Taste the fruit, and add a little sugar to start. Once it is pureed, you can add more as needed. Enhance the natural fruit flavors with a squeeze of lemon or lime juice, and a pinch of salt. If you want a super-smooth sauce, run the puree through a fine-mesh wire strainer before serving.

Grilled fruit sauces add a smoky layer of flavor that is deliciously unique. Next time you have the barbecue heated up, throw on some large slices of pineapple, some peach halves, or any other fruit you may have on hand. When they are warmed through and have good grill marks on both sides, take them off the grill and let them cool. Then proceed with the fruit sauce preparation as described above.

Chocolate Sauce

Follow the recipe for chocolate ganache (page 150), then whisk in additional liquid until you reach the desired consistency. The liquid can be cream, coffee, liquor, fruit puree, or even water.

vanilla frosting

MAKES ENOUGH FROSTING FOR 2 MUG CAKES

This frosting is terrific as is, but also provides you with a perfect blank flavor canvas on which to paint your mug cake masterpiece.

INGREDIENTS

2 tablespoons unsalted butter, softened

Pinch of kosher salt

½ teaspoon pure vanilla extract

1 teaspoon heavy cream

½ cup confectioners' sugar, sifted

METHOD

In a large mug, beat together the butter and salt with a fork until creamy. Stir in the vanilla and cream. Add the sugar and beat until smooth.

Variations

MAPLE FROSTING: Replace the vanilla extract with 1 tablespoon maple syrup. Increase the confectioners' sugar by 1 to 2 tablespoons as needed.

PEANUT BUTTER FROSTING: Replace 2 tablespoons of the softened butter with 2 tablespoons of peanut butter.

NUTELLA FROSTING: Replace 2 tablespoons of the softened butter with 2 tablespoons of Nutella. Increase the confectioners' sugar by 1 to 2 tablespoons as needed.

CITRUS FROSTING: Add the grated zest of a lemon, orange, or lime. Replace the vanilla extract with the juice of that fruit.

CARAMEL FROSTING: Replace 2 tablespoons of the softened butter with 2 tablespoons of caramel sauce. Increase the confectioners' sugar by 1 to 2 tablespoons as needed.

cream cheese frosting

This is the classic accompaniment to carrot cake and red velvet cake, but should in no way be limited to them. Try it on banana cakes, peanut butter cakes, chocolate cakes— or forgo the cake altogether and just eat it with a spoon.

INGREDIENTS

2 tablespoons (1 ounce) cream cheese, softened

1 teaspoon unsalted butter, softened

⅛ teaspoon pure vanilla extract

½ cup confectioners' sugar, sifted

Pinch of kosher salt

METHOD

In a large mug, mix together the cream cheese and butter with a fork. Add the vanilla, sugar, and salt. Beat the frosting until smooth.

Variation: There are several good-quality vegan "cream cheese" products on the market, and they all work well as a substitute in this recipe.

chocolate fudge frosting

This is a good all-purpose chocolate frosting. It's not too sweet, but it is very chocolaty.

INGREDIENTS

1 tablespoon brown sugar

1 teaspoon water

1 teaspoon corn syrup

¼ cup dark chocolate chips
(semisweet or bittersweet)

1 tablespoon unsalted
butter, softened

½ teaspoon pure vanilla
extract

½ cup confectioners' sugar,
sifted

1 tablespoon hot water
(from the tap is fine),
or as needed

METHOD

In a large mug, combine the brown sugar, water, corn syrup, chocolate chips, butter, and vanilla. Microwave the mixture for 30 to 60 seconds until it is melted. Stir with a fork until smooth. Add the confectioners' sugar, and mix with the fork until creamy. Adjust the consistency to your liking by adding a little hot water or confectioners' sugar as needed.

Variations

MOCHA FROSTING: Replace the water with an equal amount of strong brewed coffee, or espresso.

CHOCOLATE-MINT FROSTING: Add ½ teaspoon of peppermint extract in place of the vanilla.

CHOCOLATE-ORANGE FROSTING: Replace the water with an equal amount of orange liqueur. For a nonalcoholic version, use orange juice concentrate.

chocolate-sour cream frosting

MAKES ENOUGH FROSTING FOR 2 MUG CAKES

This chocolate frosting has a slight tang, thanks to the addition of sour cream. It's perfect for desserts that are already very sweet.

INGREDIENTS

¼ cup dark chocolate chips (semisweet or bittersweet)

1 tablespoon unsalted butter, softened

2 tablespoons sour cream

½ teaspoon pure vanilla extract

1 cup confectioners' sugar, sifted if possible

1 to 2 tablespoons hot water (from the tap is fine), or as needed

METHOD

In a large mug, combine the chocolate chips and butter. Microwave for 30 to 60 seconds until the mixture is melted. Stir with a fork until smooth. Stir in the sour cream and vanilla. Add the confectioners' sugar and stir with the fork until smooth. Adjust the consistency to your liking by adding a little hot water or confectioners' sugar as needed.

penuche fudge frosting

MAKES ENOUGH FROSTING FOR 2 MUG CAKES

Deep, rich brown sugar gives this frosting its charm. It adds depth and interest to mug cakes with autumnal flavors, like banana, pumpkin, date, nut, and gingerbread.

INGREDIENTS

2 tablespoons brown sugar

1 tablespoon unsalted butter, softened

1 teaspoon heavy cream

½ cup confectioners' sugar, sifted

METHOD

In a large mug, combine the brown sugar and butter. Microwave for 30 to 60 seconds until the mixture is melted. Stir in the cream. Add the confectioners' sugar and beat until smooth. Adjust the consistency to your liking by adding a little more cream or confectioners' sugar as needed.

sweetened whipped cream

MAKES 1½ CUPS WHIPPED CREAM

The French name for this all-purpose topping is *crème Chantilly*. The flavor should be subtly sweet, not cloying, because it is generally used to top desserts already sweetened. See the Variations below to change the flavor to suit any recipe. It is not possible to make this in a mug, but it is fast and easy, and totally worth the effort.

INGREDIENTS

1 cup heavy cream, well chilled

1 tablespoon granulated sugar

1 teaspoon pure vanilla extract

METHOD

In a large bowl, combine the cream, sugar, and vanilla. Using a whisk or an electric mixer, whip the cream until soft peaks appear. Watch carefully as the cream continues to stiffen, and stop when it reaches medium peaks. Overmixing is a great way to make butter.

Variations

CHOCOLATE WHIPPED CREAM: Melt ¼ cup of dark chocolate chips (semisweet or bittersweet) in the microwave for 30 to 60 seconds, then let cool to lukewarm. By hand, whisk the cooled melted chocolate into the soft-peak whipped cream until just combined. Be careful not to overwhip. (If you add the chocolate when it is hot, you will create chocolate-chip whipped cream.)

COFFEE WHIPPED CREAM: Stir 1 tablespoon of espresso powder into the cream before you begin whipping. Alternatively, fold in 1 shot of espresso, cooled, to the finished whipped cream.

COCONUT WHIPPED CREAM: Most cans of coconut milk will separate and settle as they sit on the shelf. If you avoid shaking the can, you can open it and drain off the liquid, revealing a large portion of fatty coconut paste. By hand, whisk ¼ to ½ cup of the thick coconut paste into soft peak cream until just combined. Be careful not to overwhip. (Do not discard the liquid from a can of coconut milk. That's valuable stuff! Use it in cake recipes as the liquid ingredient.) Alternatively, coconut extract can be used in place of the vanilla.

NUTELLA WHIPPED CREAM: Fold 2 to 4 tablespoons of Nutella into the soft-peak whipped cream until just combined. Be careful not to overwhip it.

CARAMEL WHIPPED CREAM: Fold 2 to 4 tablespoons of caramel sauce into the soft-peak whipped cream until just combined. Be careful not to overwhip it.

BERRY JAM WHIPPED CREAM: Fold 2 to 4 tablespoons of your favorite berry jam into the soft-peak whipped cream until just combined. To prevent clumps, stir the jam first to loosen it before adding it to the cream. Be careful not to overwhip it.

GREEN TEA WHIPPED CREAM: Stir 1 tablespoon green tea powder (instant or *macha*) into the cream before whipping. Alternatively, warm the cream and steep 1 to 2 tea bags, or the equivalent amount of loose leaves, for 30 to 40 minutes. Let cool, then whip as directed.

COLA OR ROOT BEER WHIPPED CREAM: Place 1 cup of soda pop in a saucepan and bring to a boil over high heat. Lower to a simmer, and cook until the volume is reduced by half. Cool completely, then fold it into the soft-peak whipped cream until just combined. Be careful not to overwhip it. Alternatively, add 2 to 3 drops of cola or root beer extract to the cream before whipping.

FRUIT WHIPPED CREAM: Using a blender, make a puree of firm fruit, such as berries, stone fruits, mango, papaya, or pineapple. Fold ¼ to ½ cup of the puree into the soft-peak whipped cream until just combined. Be careful not to overwhip it.

vanilla glaze

MAKES ENOUGH GLAZE FOR 2-4 MUG CAKES

INGREDIENTS

1 tablespoon unsalted butter

½ teaspoon pure vanilla extract

Pinch of kosher salt

Drop of fresh lemon juice

½ cup confectioners' sugar, sifted

1 to 2 tablespoons hot water, or as needed

METHOD

In a large mug, combine the butter, vanilla, salt, and lemon juice. Microwave for 30 seconds until the butter is melted. Add the confectioners' sugar and beat until smooth. Add hot water as needed to achieve a thin, glazelike consistency.

Variations: Any liquid flavoring can be added in place of the vanilla. Food coloring can also be added, but wait until the butter has been melted. Remember that a little food coloring goes a long way, and subtle color is always preferable. A half drop is all you'll need for this recipe, unless you need your mug cake to help guide a 747 in for a landing.

HONEY GLAZE: Replace the vanilla extract with 1 teaspoon of honey. Increase the confectioners' sugar by 1 to 2 tablespoons, or as needed.

AGAVE GLAZE: Replace the vanilla extract with 1 teaspoon of agave. Increase the confectioners' sugar by 1 to 2 tablespoons as needed. For agave-lime glaze, add the zest of 1 lime and a tablespoon of lime juice as well. Increase the confectioners' sugar by 2 to 4 tablespoons, or as needed.

RUM GLAZE: Replace the vanilla extract with 2 tablespoons of dark rum, and increase the confectioners' sugar by 1 to 2 tablespoons, or as needed. Alternatively, replace the vanilla extract with rum extract. Use the same procedure, using any other brandy or liqueur.

CARAMEL GLAZE: Reduce the butter to 1 teaspoon, and add 2 tablespoons of caramel sauce to the mug. Microwave them together until they are soft and liquefied, then proceed with the recipe as written. You can also add brandy or another liqueur in place of the hot water

MAPLE GLAZE: Reduce the butter to 1 teaspoon and add 2 tablespoons of maple syrup to the mug. Microwave them together until they are soft and liquefied, then proceed with the recipe as written.

SOUR CREAM GLAZE: Reduce the butter to 1 teaspoon. After the butter is melted, stir in 2 tablespoons of sour cream, then proceed with the recipe as written.

LEMON GLAZE: Reduce the butter to 1 teaspoon. After the butter is melted, stir in the finely grated zest of 1 lemon and 2 tablespoons of fresh lemon juice. Proceed with the recipe as written. This same method can be used for any citrus fruit.

FRUIT GLAZE: Reduce the butter to 1 teaspoon. After the butter is melted, stir in 2 tablespoons of fruit jam or fruit puree, then proceed with the recipe as written. (Use a blender to make a puree from firm fruit, such as berries, stone fruits, mango, papaya, or pineapple.)

APPLE GLAZE: Reduce the butter to 1 teaspoon and add 2 tablespoons of apple juice concentrate. Microwave them together until they are soft and liquefied, then proceed with the recipe as written.

COCONUT GLAZE: Reduce the butter to 1 teaspoon. After the butter is melted, stir in 2 tablespoons of unsweetened coconut milk, then proceed with the recipe as written.

RUM-RAISIN GLAZE: Reduce the butter to 1 teaspoon. Add 1 tablespoon of dark rum and 2 tablespoons of raisins. Microwave these together, then set aside for 10 to 15 minutes to plump. Proceed with the recipe as written. (Use this method with dark raisins, golden raisins, currants, or any other dried fruit you'd like.)

chocolate ganache

MAKES 1 CUP GANACHE

This classic recipe is the base of dozens of desserts, and it is a staple ingredient in every professional pastry kitchen. Chilled and rolled, it is the center of a truffle. Poured hot over cakes, it is a shiny glaze. Whipped stiff, it makes a pretty frosting. Allowed to set slowly at room temperature, it is the perfect filling. Because of this versatility, I encourage you to make a larger batch to keep on hand as an impressive finishing touch to any dessert you make. It will keep beautifully in the fridge for a week or two, and in the freezer for even longer.

INGREDIENTS

½ cup heavy cream

¾ cup dark chocolate chips
(semisweet or bittersweet)

METHOD

In a large mug, microwave the cream for 30 to 60 seconds until very hot. Add the chocolate chips, taking care to ensure that they are all submerged. Let the mixture stand at room temperature for 10 to 15 minutes. After the rest period, beat the ganache with a fork until smooth.

Note: If this is being made on the stovetop, bring the cream to a boil before pouring it over the chocolate chips.

Variations

MILK CHOCOLATE GANACHE: Because milk chocolate contains more fat than dark chocolate, this recipe requires more chocolate than cream. The higher fat content also means that it is more sensitive to heat and can burn easily. Use 1½ cups of milk chocolate chips or chunks. If the heat of the cream does not melt all of the chocolate, microwave the entire recipe in 5-second increments, beating with the fork each time, until all of the chocolate is melted.

WHITE CHOCOLATE GANACHE: White chocolate ganache also contains more fat than dark chocolate, so this recipe also requires more chocolate than cream. And again, the higher fat content means that it is more sensitive to heat, and can burn easily. Use 1 cup of white chocolate chips or chunks and ¼ cup heavy cream. If the heat of the cream does not melt all of the chocolate, microwave the entire recipe in 5-second increments, beating with the fork each time, until all of the chocolate is melted.

caramel sauce

Caramel sauce is easily bought ready-made. But if you are the adventurous type, this is a must-have pastry technique. The finished sauce will keep for weeks in the refrigerator, and can be enhanced a dozen ways to suit your mood and your mug. It can't be made in a mug, but why let that stop you?

INGREDIENTS

2 cups granulated sugar

¼ cup water, plus more as needed

1 tablespoon fresh lemon juice

1½ cups heavy cream

4 tablespoons (½ stick) unsalted butter

Variations: Classic additions include vanilla extract, vanilla bean, espresso, instant coffee powder, peanut butter, Nutella, melted chocolate, Scotch whiskey (for butterscotch sauce), champagne, cider, or balsamic vinegar, and fleur de sel. It's always best to start small and then add more as needed.

METHOD

In a large saucepan, combine the sugar and the water. Using your fingertips, mix it together, then use a little extra water to wipe all stray sugar crystals off the sides of the pan. Place the pan over high heat and cook the mixture without stirring.

When the mixture reaches a rolling boil, add the lemon juice to the center of the pot. Do not stir it at all—the bubbles will do that for you. Continue cooking, without stirring, until the sugar is a dark, golden amber.

Remove the pot from the heat and whisk in the cream. When the cream is added, it will erupt like a volcano. Stand back, and watch out for the steam. (Some people like to wear a big oven mitt for this step.) Whisking will cool it, and calm it down quickly. If there are lumps after the cream is added, return it to the stove and stir over low heat until they dissolve.

Add the butter and whisk the sauce until smooth. Cool to room temperature before serving or storing.

hard sauce

MAKES 1 CUP HARD SAUCE

This is the most decadent topping you can imagine. Its name is a diversion, meant to keep its luscious secret for only those with an adventurous spirit. Hard sauce gets hard when it is chilled, but it is better served fresh, a generous plop on top of a cake pulled steaming hot from the oven. This recipe calls for brandy, but you can use any booze you choose. For the best results, add it a little at a time, letting it slowly emulsify.

INGREDIENTS

4 tablespoons (½ stick) unsalted butter, softened

¾ cup confectioners' sugar, sifted

Pinch of kosher salt

1 tablespoon brandy

METHOD

Place the softened butter in a large mug and mix it with a fork until creamy. Add the sugar and beat until smooth. Stir in the salt and brandy, and mix until the sauce is creamy and well combined.

lemon curd

MAKES 3–4 CUPS (OR ABOUT 1 QUART) CURD

Lemon curd appears in the recipe for Lemon Mug Bars, and can be made in small batches in the microwave. But this is another recipe that is so easy and good that it pays to make it in a larger batch. It can be used not only as a topping for your mug cake, but as a filling for tart, pies, or as it was originally intended, as a spread for toast and scones.

INGREDIENTS

6 *whole large eggs*

5 *large egg yolks*

1¾ *cups granulated sugar*

Finely grated zest of 4 lemons

1⅓ *cups fresh lemon juice*

16 *tablespoons (2 sticks) unsalted butter*

METHOD

In a large saucepan, combine the whole eggs, yolks, sugar, lemon zest, lemon juice, salt, and butter. Whisk them together and set the pan over high heat.

Stir continuously with a heatproof spatula or wooden spoon until the mixture thickens to a sour cream consistency. Strain the thickened curd immediately through fine-mesh wire into a clean bowl. Cover it with plastic wrap, pressed directly on the surface. Cool it to room temperature before serving or storing.

Variation: Curd needs adequate acid to thicken. It is easily made with lime juice instead of lemons, but for orange, cranberry, or pomegranate curd, adjustments must be made. Use ⅓ cup of lemon juice, and replace the rest with the less acidic juice.

candied citrus peel

MAKES ½ CUP CITRUS PEEL

This is one of the most impressive garnishes you can serve. Secretly, it is also crazy-easy. Make more than you need and keep in the freezer for impromptu showing off.

INGREDIENTS

4 cups water

½ cup citrus peel strips

1 cup granulated sugar

Note: The citrus peel should have a little white pith attached, but not much. A channel knife is the best tool for this. It is like a citrus zester, but instead of having four tiny holes, there is only one large hole. Drawn across the rind, it digs out a long strip of peel, about ¼ inch thick. If you don't have this tool, just remove some peel and cut it into strips with a sharp knife.

METHOD

In a small saucepan, bring 3 cups of water to a rolling boil. Add the peel and blanch it by cooking it at the boil for 1 to 2 minutes. This will remove any bitterness. Strain the peel and discard the blanching water.

In a small saucepan (use the same one if you want), combine the sugar and the remaining water and bring it to a boil over high heat. Add the blanched zest and reduce the heat to a bare simmer. Simmer the zest for 30 to 60 minutes until it begins to turn translucent and is tender to the touch. Drain off the sugar syrup (you may want to save it for a yummy sauce) and spread the zest out on a plate or pan to cool. Serve as is, or toss it in granulated sugar for a frosted effect.

Variation: This method of candying also works with carrot strips (peeled off the carrot in thick ribbons using a potato peeler) and with fresh ginger (sliced in sticks, coins, or removed in ribbons with a peeler).

candied nuts

There is nothing quite as satisfactory as the crunch of a salty nut coated in crisp, cara-melized sugar. Well, there might be a lot of things that good, but the point is, you should try these, too.

INGREDIENTS

1½ cups nuts (pecan halves, walnut halves, macadamias, peanuts, or cashews)

¼ cup packed brown sugar

1 teaspoon kosher salt

2 tablespoons unsalted butter

METHOD

In a small bowl, combine the nuts, sugar, and salt. Toss them together so they are well coated.

Melt the butter in a large sauté pan over medium heat. When it starts to sizzle, add the nut mixture. Stir constantly for 3 to 5 minutes until the sugar has melted and the nuts are toasted. Pour them out immediately onto a baking sheet in a single layer and cool completely.

Variation: Spice up these nuts by adding ground cinnamon, cayenne pepper, white pepper, or ground fennel. Toss the spices with the nuts, sugar, and salt before cooking.

streusel

MAKES 2 CUPS STREUSEL

Streusel, also known as crisp, crumb, or crumble topping, is easy to whip up and great to have on hand. It keeps for weeks in the freezer, and can be used to top not only mug cakes and pies, but in standard baking recipes as well, like muffins and coffee cakes. I encourage you to make a big batch so you are always streusel-ready.

INGREDIENTS

1 cup all-purpose flour

½ cup granulated sugar

½ cup unsalted butter, chilled and diced

METHOD

In a large bowl, mix together the flour and sugar. Add the butter, and using your fingertips or a fork, work it until it is broken down into very small pieces. The streusel is ready when it resembles a coarse meal. It should hold together when squeezed, but easily crumble apart. Be careful not to overmix it, or the streusel will become gummy when cooked.

Crumble the streusel on top of the item to be baked, and proceed as directed. Store leftover streusel in the freezer for up to 1 month.

Variations: Streusel can be made with brown sugar, white sugar, or a combination. It can also be made with whole wheat flour, or any gluten-free flour instead of all-purpose flour. You can add up to ½ cup of finely chopped nuts of your choice, ½ cup of rolled oats, and 2 to 3 teaspoons of your favorite spices.

sautéed fruit

Warm caramelized fruit is a wonderful topping and works with just about any fruit you can imagine. It can't be made in a mug, but is an easy technique, and can turn an ordinary dessert into a "Wow!" Use this technique to cook firm fruits like apples, pears, bananas, pineapple, or peaches.

INGREDIENTS

½ cup granulated sugar

Pinch of kosher salt

2 cups sliced fruit

2 tablespoons unsalted butter

Variation: This method works equally well with brown sugar, which lends a rich, molasses flavor.

METHOD

In a small bowl, combine the sugar, salt, and fruit. Toss them together so the fruit is well coated.

Melt the butter in a large sauté pan over medium heat. When it starts to sizzle, add the fruit mixture. Stir constantly for 3 to 5 minutes until the sugar has melted and begun to caramelize. Pour the fruit out immediately onto a plate and cool slightly before serving.

glossary

add-ins A term referring to garnishes folded into dough and batter, such as chocolate chips, nuts, or raisins.

amaretto An Italian liqueur with the distinctive flavor of bitter almonds.

anise An annual flowering herb, related to parsley. The seeds have a distinctive licorice flavor, which is used in liqueurs, candies, sauces, and cosmetics.

blanch To boil briefly, then submerge in ice water to halt the cooking. The process is used to loosen the skin and intensify the color of vegetables and fruits. Also referred to as *parboiling*.

cajeta A Mexican caramel made from goat's milk. It is available as a sauce in jars and bottles, and as a candy, ready to eat.

candied ginger Fresh ginger, cooked in sugar syrup, and coated in sugar, used in baked goods.

caramelized To cook food until the sugar, naturally occurring or added, darkens to an amber caramel color. Caramelization brings out a food's deep, sweet, rich flavors.

cassis A liqueur made from the blackcurrant, and sold under the name crème de cassis, it is produced famously in Burgundy, Anjou, and Luxembourg.

clotted cream Thick cream from unpasteurized milk. Also known as Devonshire cream.

Cointreau An orange-flavored brandy made in France.

crema A Mexican soured cream, with a more delicate flavor and thinner consistency than sour cream.

crème fraîche A French thickened cream with a slightly tangy flavor. It has a higher butterfat content and thicker consistency than sour cream.

crumble A dessert also known as a crisp, consisting of fruit baked with a streusel topping.

currants Tiny raisins made from miniature Zante grapes. Do not confuse them with red, white, or black currants, which are small berries used for preserves, pastries, and the liqueur *cassis*.

filberts Another name for hazelnuts.

ganache A pastry kitchen staple, made from equal parts cream and chocolate, which is used for fillings, truffles, glazes, and icings.

gluten The protein in wheat endosperm that promotes elasticity in bread dough. When moistened and agitated, gluten proteins tighten, creating a smooth, firm dough that can stretch to hold the gas of fermentation.

macerate To soak food, usually fruit, in liquid to infuse flavor.

microplane A fine rasp grater used for grating citrus zest and hard cheeses. The tool was originally a carpenter's rasp used for sanding wood, then was trademarked and marketed as a Microplane.

nutella An Italian butter made from ground hazelnuts and milk chocolate. Nutella was first developed in World War II as a way to extend rationed chocolate.

pasilla Sometimes referred to as *chile negro*, the pasilla was traditionally a dried chilaca pepper. In the United States the pasilla is usually a dried poblano or ancho pepper.

reduce A culinary term meaning to cook the water out of a dish, reducing its volume, intensifying its flavor, and thickening its consistency.

rancid Oxidation of oil that results in foul flavor and odor.

saturated fat Fatty acids fully saturated with hydrogen. These fats are solid at room temperature, and are mainly found in animal sources, although oil from coconut, cotton, and palm contains high percentages of saturated fatty acids. Intake should be limited to no more than 7 percent of total daily calories, as saturated fat has been shown to be a major cause of coronary artery disease.

sauté To cook food quickly, over high heat, constantly stirring for even browning. The term means "to jump" and sauté pans are designed with a curved lip, making constant motion as easy as a flick of the wrist.

sriracha sauce A Vietnamese hot chile sauce made with vinegar, garlic, and salt. It is often called "rooster sauce" in the United States, in reference to the rooster on the label of the best-selling brand, Huy Fong.

stone fruit A tree fruit that contains a pit, or stone, such as peaches, apricots, cherries, and plums.

tabasco A small red pepper from the Mexican state of Tabasco, grown in Louisiana by the McIlhenny Company specifically for the production of Tabasco sauce.

Triple Sec A clear orange-flavored liqueur.

unsaturated A fat that remains liquid when refrigerated. These fats include polyunsaturated and monounsaturated and are found in plant foods such as olives, avocados, soy, nuts, and canola.

zest The colorful outermost rind of a citrus fruit, containing a high concentration of the essential oils and flavor compounds that flavor the fruit itself.

zester A small tool designed to strip the aromatic, colorful, oil-rich skin from citrus fruit. Often made with four holes.

common
food substitutions

baking powder, 1 teaspoon, can be replaced by: ¼ teaspoon baking soda plus ⅝ teaspoon cream of tartar, or ¼ teaspoon baking soda plus ½ cup buttermilk

buttermilk, 1 cup, can be replaced by: 1 cup yogurt, or 1 cup milk plus 1 tablespoon lemon juice, or 1 cup milk plus 1 tablespoon vinegar, or 1 cup milk plus 1 teaspoon cream of tartar

cake flour, 1 cup, can be replaced by: 1 cup all-purpose flour plus 1 tablespoon cornstarch

cornstarch, 1 tablespoon, can be replaced by: 2 tablespoons all-purpose flour

corn syrup, 1 cup, can be replaced by: 1¼ cups sugar plus ¼ cup water

cream, 1 cup, can be replaced by: ¾ cup whole milk plus ⅓ cup butter

egg, 1 whole, can be replaced by: 2 yolks, or 2 whites, or 3½ tablespoons egg substitute

egg white, 1, can be replaced by: 1 tablespoon powdered egg white, or 2 tablespoons frozen egg whites

egg yolk, 1, can be replaced by: 2 tablespoons powdered yolk, or 3½ teaspoons frozen yolk

honey, 1 cup, can be replaced by: 1¼ cups white sugar, and increasing recipe liquid by ¼ cup

milk, 1 cup, can be replaced by: ½ cup evaporated milk plus ½ cup water, or ¼ cup powdered milk plus ⅔ cup water

common food approximate volume equivalents

apples, 1 pound, is equivalent to 3 cups sliced

bananas, 1 pound, is equivalent to 2 cups sliced, 1½ cups mashed

butter, 1 pound, is equivalent to 2 cups

carrots, 1 pound, is equivalent to 3 cups chopped

chocolate chips, 6 ounces, is equivalent to 1 cup

cornmeal, 1 pound, is equivalent to 3 cups

cornstarch, 1 pound, is equivalent to 3 cups

cream, liquid, 1 cup, is equivalent to 2 cups whipped

egg whites, 1 cup, is equivalent to 8 medium

egg yolks, 1 cup, is equivalent to 12 medium

flour, all-purpose, 1 pound, is equivalent to 4 cups

flour, bread, unsifted, 1 pound, is equivalent to 3 cups

flour, cake, unsifted, 1 pound, is equivalent to 4½ cups

gelatin, unflavored, ¼ ounces, is equivalent to 1 tablespoon or 3½ sheets

graham crackers, 16 squares, is equivalent to 1 cup crumbs

lemons, 6 to 7 fruits, is equivalent to 1 cup juice

limes, 1 to 2 fruits, is equivalent to 1 tablespoon juice

marshmallows, 1 pound, is equivalent to 60 large

nuts, chopped, 1 pound, is equivalent to 3½ cups

oats, 1 pound, is equivalent to 5 cups

pumpkin, canned, 17 ounces, is equivalent to 2 cups puree

pumpkin, fresh, 1 pound, is equivalent to 1 cup puree

raisins, 1 pound, is equivalent to 3 cups

rhubarb, fresh, 1 pound, is equivalent to 2 cups chopped

sugar, brown, 1 pound, is equivalent to 2⅓ cups, packed

sugar, confectioners', 1 pound, is equivalent to 3¾ cups, unsifted

sugar, granulated, 1 pound, is equivalent to 2¼ cups

yeast, dry, 1 (¼ ounce) package, is equivalent to 2½ teaspoons

acknowledgments

Thanks to everyone at St. Martin's Press, including the amazing design team, Jasmine Faustino, and especially my editor, BJ Berti. It has been a real pleasure.

A big thank-you to everyone who sacrificed their time and waistlines to test out mug cakes—Jerry and Lori, the many mug testers at St. Martin's Press, Michael Harants (it's the thought that counts), my mommy, Kristi Rodehorst, and especially Emma and Claire, who are my toughest critics (in a good way). Thanks to Katherine Latshaw for planting the seed. And most of all, thanks to Bill, my best friend and biggest fan.

index